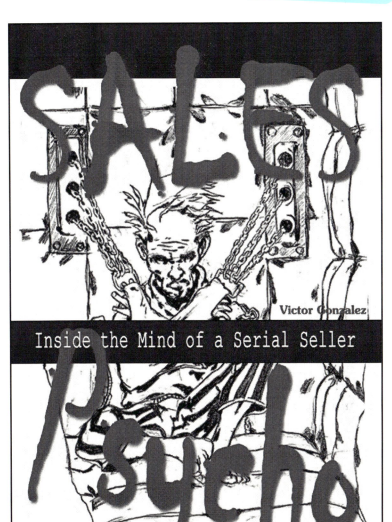

SALES

Psycho

Victor Gonzalez

Inside the Mind of a Serial Seller

The Sales Asylum
You Have to be Committed to Get In

Sales Psycho

Inside the Mind of a
Serial Seller

By Victor Gonzalez

1st Edition

Battle Elf Publishing

This Battle Elf Publication Edition is by published by
Victor Gonzalez, The Sales Asylum
11770 Haynes Bridge Road
Suite 205-501
Alpharetta, Georgia 30004
www.victorgonzalez.com

Printed in the United States of America
First Printing: August 2007

Library of Congress Cataloging in Publication Data
Gonzalez, Victor
        Sales Psycho – Inside the Mind of a Serial Seller

ISBN 0-9768840-6-2
ISBN 978-0-9768840-6-4 (U.S.A.)

1. Business 2. Success

Dedicated to my Father

September 3, 1932 – May 18, 2000

The Good Really Die Young!

Every crime has a motive. Every sale has a profit motive!

Victor Gonzalez, 2007

Born and raised in one of Chicago's worst inner cities, Victor Gonzalez has achieved a level of success few expected.

By age 35 he was Vice President in a $3B Fortune 500 Company, then President of Global Sales & Marketing to help build a $420M company. He went on to become a CEO in a high tech company. Not bad for someone whose family depended on food stamps and government handouts growing up. A living testimonial of persistence and overcoming adversity!

A dynamic, keynote speaker with a Bachelors Degree in Electrical Engineering and MBA, Victor keynotes at corporations on "The Logic of Sales Success".

For more information on Victor go to:
www.VictorGonzalez.com

SALES ASYLUM

You Have to be Committed to Get In

CONFIDENTIAL

INSTITUTION: SALES ASYLUM

CASE#: SS0107

INMATE: CLASSIFIED

DOB: UNKNOWN

SECTOR: M BLOCK

CATEGORY: SERIAL SELLER

ACCESS: GRANTED

PURPOSE: INTERVIEW

SPECIAL INSTRUCTIONS:
STRAITJACKET AND CHAIN RESTRAINTS
REQUIRED FOR INMATE PRIOR TO INTERVIEW.
INTERVIEWER MUST NOT ATTEMPT ANY
PHYSICAL CONTACT AND SHOULD MAINTAIN
APPROPRIATE DISTANCE.

INSIDE THE ASYLUM

"Entering Sector: M Block," the sign reads. I'm being directed toward a door to my immediate left. The guard instructs me to wait as he unlocks the door, steps inside and closes the door behind him. Moments later the door reopens and the guard invites me to come inside.

The room is blinding white, and my eyes take a while to adjust. It's a padded room, square, with white cushioned panels covering the walls. The ceiling is a sheet of corrugated grey steel with a single air duct to pipe heat or cool air into the room.

The floor is a uniform mattress, the kind you see in those foam mattress commercials. Once inside, I have no sense of the front or back of the room.

I notice the man bound in a straitjacket sitting on the foam floor against the wall, across from where I came in. His legs are crossed and his head tilted up. His gaze is focused on the air duct overhead. He stares as if waiting for something or someone to come out of it. The duct itself is no more than six inches wide. Maybe the noise of the air rushing through the duct is captivating his attention.

I lean over to the guard and quietly ask, "Is that him?" He nods as we approach the center of the room. "You have two hours for your interview," he states. He hands me a remote control. "If you need us to come in for any reason, press the red button on this control. We'll be in here faster than you can sneeze." He informs me that the

10

only way to open the door is from the
outside, by one of the orderlies on duty.

As he closes the door behind him, a look of
concern comes over his face. "Remember,
he's still unstable. Even though he is
restrained, he can still be dangerous, so
be careful not to get too close to him."

The door shuts with a dull thud and
literally disappears into the padded wall.
I feel a slight anxiety, wondering if I
could find it again if I needed to.

Turning back toward Patient SS0107, I see
he is still fixated on the overhead duct. I
move toward him but stop near the center of
the room. His straitjacket is shackled with
chains to bolt loops protruding from the
wall behind him.

Judging by the length of the chains, I feel
safe at this distance. I pull out my
digital recorder and notepad and prepare
for the interview.

INTERVIEW: SS0107

ENTRY DATE: UNKNOWN

Transcript Note > To my knowledge, this is the first documented interview with a Serial Seller. What you are about to read is the full transcript from this interview.

V: Hi, my name is Victor. How are you doing today?

SS: That's a dumbass question. Hmmm, let me see. I'm in a padded room, in straitjacket and chained to a wall. I'm doing marvelous, you idiot!

V: Just trying to be polite.

SS: I don't care what you're trying to be.

V: Alright, let's start again. I'm here to interview you. May we begin?

SS: Your tone sounds more sincere.

V: What was wrong with my tone in my opening question?

SS: It sounded canned, like you didn't give a damn how I really felt. It was just a question you had to ask for the sake of asking it.

V: My apologies. I'll try to watch my tone in the future.

SS: You're doing it again. You sound like a cardboard cutout of Mr. Rogers.

V: What's your problem?

SS: I don't have a problem, you do.

V: What's that?

SS: Authenticity. If you're going to come in here and open a conversation, at least have the decency to pretend you care. Or is this going to be an interrogation and not an interview?

V: What the difference?

SS: You're kidding, right? You must be new at this. An interrogation is usually a one way conversation. An interview is a conversation between two people. So are you here to talk with me or AT me?

V: I want to talk with you. I want to find out what made you a Serial Seller.

SS: A what?

V: A Serial Seller. You know, someone obsessed with selling. And, if I may be so blunt, I don't want canned answers either. I'd like real answers to tough questions from a person who apparently was at the top of his sales game. How's my tone now?

SS: A little pissed off, but I like it. It sounds honest. And what do you mean, 'was' at the top of the sales game? I can still outsell anyone out there today. Let me out and I'll prove it. I'm the best.

V: If I didn't think you were the best, why would I be here?

SS: Flattery, huh? Maybe you're not as dumb as you seem. Okay. Where do you want to start?

V: Well, now that we've kissed and made up, why don't we start at the beginning?

Transcript Note > Beginning interview after rough introduction. Looking for how SS became interested in selling.

V: When did you know you wanted to be in sales? Was it an early childhood desire? What was it that made you go into selling?

SS: First of all, let's not be so melodramatic about it. Growing up, I never even knew there existed this thing called sales, or selling.

V: Surely someone in your childhood sold you something, or maybe your parents?

SS: (pause) Well, there was this man who sold my mother plastic covers for our sofas. You know, back then people used to cover their sofas with plastic to make them last longer.

V: Plastic covers on your sofas? Sounds strange!

SS: When you're poor and you invest in something like furniture, you want it to last until your kids leave the house. My mother wasn't taking any chances with seven of us in the house.

V: Seven! Wow!

SS: Anyway, I remember they were expensive because my father was always concerned about the cost and complaining to my mother. My father worked in a factory busting his ass for little or no money, while Mom's job was to take care of all seven of us. I don't know who had it worse, my father killing himself at the factory or Mom trying to raise seven hellions.

V: What about this plastic cover salesman?

SS: Well, he came over with a bunch of sample coverings. Some were clear plastic, but the more expensive ones were cloth fabric with paisley designs on them. I remember my mother choosing the clear plastic covers. The salesman then measured the sofa and promised delivery a few weeks later. My mother gave him something like $20 as good faith money. That may not seem like a lot of money, but back then it was, because it always seemed we were just getting by. My mother spent the next year paying off those covers. Every week the man would come by to collect his fee. If that was selling, screw that. I remember this poor guy having to go around collecting his money from our neighbors, many who had excuses why they couldn't pay him.

V: I couldn't imagine that working today. Everything today is done either online or on the phone with a credit card. If you think about it, it's amazing how far we've come in terms of technology.

SS: Yeah, but sales hasn't changed. It's still the same as it was back then.

V: You think so?

SS: I know so.

V: Can you remember your first sales experience?

SS: I don't know. Let me think for a second here. (pause) There were two childhood experiences that molded my take on selling. Now that I really think of it, they were probably the same reasons I never considered a life in selling.

V: What were they? Tell me about them.

SS: Careful, dude. You're starting to go into shrink mode again with the canned responses.

V: Didn't mean to.

SS: Whatever. When I was around 12 or 13, my parents encouraged me to get a newspaper route. Remember when newspapers were delivered with a bike and not a car? When you would strap the newspaper bag on your bike's handlebars and go? I remember being excited. I would get up at 3 or 4 in the morning to go pick up the newspapers at the office. We had to fold and rubber-band our own papers, stuff them in the bag and then head out. Each of us had a giant ring with about 50 pink tags; each tag represented a house where we had to drop off the newspaper.

V: Did you enjoy doing that?

SS: At first, yeah, it was exciting. My first real paying job, or so I thought. When I was recruited to deliver papers, no one said I'd also have to collect the money. It was tough at first finding the houses and then doing my best to avoid getting bit by their dogs when I delivered. I remember at the end of the first month I went to collect. I came back with about 50% of the houses collected. I'd bang on doors, ring door bells, but no one would answer. We were paid on what we collected. I remember getting paid $25 for a whole month's worth of work. Man, that sucked! For one whole month of getting up at 4 in the morning, all I had to show was $25. That came out to less than a dollar a day. I was done. I handed in my newspaper bag and called it quits.

V: Some would say you gave up.

SS: Some can kiss my ass! I was poor, not stupid. The math didn't add up. What really pissed me off were those deadbeats who never paid. I went back to a few of those houses often to collect. They still weren't home. I found out that certain routes were loaded with deadbeats who hadn't paid their newspaper bill for at least a month or two, if not more.

V: So you did learn something about sales.

SS: What? That people hate paying their bills?! Dude, I didn't need a worthless paper route to tell me that. I could've just turned to my family members for that piece of datum.

V: No, that's not what I was referring to. You learned if you have a poor territory, your sales numbers won't be so great. Poor territory meant poor commissions. You also learned about accounts payable and delinquent payments.

SS: (Looking at me, eyes wide) Son of a bitch! I never thought of that. That's fucking genius on your part because up till now I never looked at it that way! Ha! I guess imprinting does begin early.

V: We're all conditioned by our environment, whether we're conscious of it or not.

SS: Back off professor, you're going deep on me, and I barely have my toe in the water here.

V: Backing off! Backing off! What was the other experience you were referring to? You mentioned two childhood experiences?

SS: Well, this one was when I was younger. I don't remember the exact age, but I'm going to guess around 10. My friend Gooch, that was his last name, and I decided to set up a lemonade and candy stand on the side of the road. We went to the corner candy store called Mitchell's to get our supplies.

V: Was Mitchell a real person or just a name?

SS: No, Mr. Mitchell was very real. Him and his wife ran this little candy-grocery store on the corner of North Avenue and Ashland Avenue in Chicago. I grew up with Mr. Mitchell. My father and mother knew him. When we didn't have any money for milk or bread, Mr. and Mrs. Mitchell gave us groceries on credit. My father would pay him without fail. My father, God bless him, never stiffed anyone. He would give his last dollar to anyone who really needed it.

V: Is your father still alive?

SS: (long pause) So that morning, me and Gooch went and bought a mix of candy and Kool-Aid powder packets to sell on our street. You know, those were the days when a 10-year-old could walk to the corner store without any fear of sexual predators and the like. Times have changed.

V: I do know what you mean. So what did you do after you bought your supplies?

SS: I can still see us today with an old milk carton turned sideways as our table and countertop along the street curb. Our bought candy displayed like a deck of cards, along with a pitcher of red-cherry Kool-Aid for sale. I don't remember what we priced the items at, but I do remember that no one was stopping to buy. I think we stood out in that hot sun for a good half-hour before we started to sample the merchandise. We didn't sell anything that day, and I remember us finally deciding to pack it in and find a shady spot to liquidate our inventory!

V: Were you disappointed that no one stopped to buy from you?

SS: I honestly can't remember. But even today I have an aversion to holding a garage sale; maybe that had something to do with it. There's something about waiting, waiting for someone to show up and decide to buy. If it did teach me something, it taught me that I hate waiting for someone to show up to buy.

V: So do you think it taught you to be more proactive when it comes to selling?

SS: C'mon! I was ten, for God's sake. The only thing it taught me was that selling on a hot day sucked but that you can still enjoy your spoils if you don't sell. Not selling wasn't a bad thing that day. It was a good thing.

V: Yes, but you didn't make any money?

SS: Who gave a rip at the time! We were kids. This may come as a shock to you, but the profit motive wasn't instilled in all of us at the age of 10. If I remember correctly, we used Gooch's money which copped from his mother's quarter jar.

V: Quarter jar?

SS: Yeah, Gooch's mother had this big jar where she would put all her twenty-five cent pieces. Gooch copped a few thinking she wouldn't notice – which she didn't until much later, and that's a whole other story. So no, it didn't cost me anything.

V: Didn't you feel bad for your friend Gooch?

SS: Not that I remember. Gooch wasn't the brightest bulb on his family tree, and it wasn't the first time he was hoodwinked.

V: Do you think that experience formed you in any way?

SS: What do you mean, 'formed me?'

V: Did it impact you in the way you approach selling today?

SS: No clue. You'll have to put me under and tap into my psyche for that answer. But now that you mention it, maybe it taught me to always use other people's money to finance a venture if they're naïve enough to go along with it! (Laughs)

V: You never answered my question.

SS: Which one?

V: Is your father still alive?

SS: No, he isn't, so let's drop it.

V: Why?

SS: Because it's not relevant to what you're looking for.

V: And what am I looking for?

SS: Fuck you! You know what! You're here to find out what makes me a Serial Seller. How I outsell my competition. What drives me to be the best at what I do and what makes me tick harder than the other clocks out there. Am I right?

V: Yes.

SS: Then let's move on. My father has nothing to do with this conversation.

V: Now who's being disingenuous? You honestly expect me to believe that your father made no impact on your life? You want me to believe that a man who supported you didn't contribute anything to who you are today? That's bullshit, and you know it!

SS: (Glaring) Tell you what. Let's get through this interview, and at the end I'll tell you just exactly how my father molded me. Because even if I wanted to tell you now, which I don't, I'm not sure you'd understand. Agreed?

V: Agreed. I'm willing to wait. But you have to agree not to cheat me out of my answer. I want it all. No holding back! Agreed?

SS: Done.

V: So take me back to the first sales job you had and how it came about.

SS: Well, I didn't think about being in sales, it kind of just happened. I was in technical support for a company that developed wireless systems. My job was to put together designs for companies who wanted to build their own communications network.

V: Did you have a technical background?

SS: Yes, I went to college and graduated with a Bachelor's Degree in Electrical Engineering.

V: I didn't know that. Now you've piqued my curiosity. How did you get from engineering to sales?

SS: I decided to get an engineering degree not because I loved engineering, but because I heard engineers got paid great money. We were poor, so I was looking for a way to ensure that once I graduated I would be making good money.

V: Did you graduate with good grades?

SS: Nah. I graduated with a 2.63 GPA. Not bad, C-plus average.

V: Hey, you made it through, that's what counts.

SS: So glad you approve. I once read that the average millionaire in the U.S. has a C-plus average. If that's true, I'm in good company.

V: So after graduation, you started working as an engineer.

SS: Yeah. I soon realized I didn't like it. Something about sitting in front of computers and electronic equipment wasn't for me.

V: So how did you get into sales?

SS: I kept moving around trying to find my 'true calling,' if you will. I went from engineer to technical support and then customer support. One day I was offered a job to work for a company as an application engineer putting together wireless networks. My job would be to support the sales team when it came to doing presentations.

V: So you started doing presentations early on in your career?

SS: (Nods) At first it was intimidating. Our systems were expensive; I'm talking millions of dollars. Many of my big presentations were in front of high level executives who were making the buying decisions. So you can imagine the pressure not to screw up. Salesmen were the worst. If you screwed up a presentation in front of the potential buyer, you can bet everyone back at the home office would find out about it. So the goal was not to screw up.

V: If you did screw up?

SS: Well, if you got the reputation for screwing up, the company would keep you 'in-house' – they would never send you out on presentations. Sometimes the salesmen would have an informal black list of engineers they didn't want to invite to do presentations. If you were on that list, it wasn't good.

V: Did you ever get on that list?

SS: Hell, no! I was not only good technically, my presentation skills rivaled the best salesman's at the time.

V: A little cocky, weren't you?

SS: Cocky is not being able to back it up. I knew I was better; I call that confidence with skills to back it up.

V: Well, you did graduate with a C average.

SS: You're a funny guy! Ha, ha!

Transcript Note > Interviewee discusses developing his front-of-the-room presentation skills. Attributes a great deal of his success to this area. Confidence is very noticeable.

V: Where did you get your presentation skills?

SS: What I didn't tell a lot of people is that I had joined this organization called Toastmasters. Have you heard of it?

V: No.

SS: It's an organization with local chapters throughout the U.S. aimed at helping people develop their speaking skills. I had heard about this organization a few years back and decided to look into it. I did, I liked what I saw and I joined.

V: So they teach you how to present?

SS: When you join, you're given the task of delivering ten different types of presentations, each 5-7 minutes long - over a period of time, not in one day. When you present, your peers evaluate you and give you feedback on how to improve. My first presentation wasn't horrible, but it wasn't pretty. By the time I got to speech number ten, I was pretty damn good. So much so that we had an internal competition, and I beat their top speaker. From there I started competing locally and statewide and I cleaned up pretty good. I won a lot of trophies.

V: Is that when you got the sales itch?

SS: That experience with Toastmasters proved to me I could present with the best

26

of them. Traveling around with the salespeople further convinced me that I could be just as good, if not better than most. That's when I started to get the sales itch. The more I hung around the salesmen, supporting them in their sales efforts, the more I started to like what I heard and the lifestyle they led.

V: Lifestyle?

SS: You know, no more 'nine to five.' These salesmen dressed better than most, drove better cars and seem to be happier. What I really liked was not having a structure.

V: You mean not having your job structured?

SS: Exactly. In sales, you were the person that made up your schedule. You were the architect of your own success.

V: You're starting to sound like a motivational speaker.

SS: Kiss my ass. By 'architect,' I mean you were in control, to the extent you could control things, of how your day or week or month went. Upper management gave these guys a quota and said, Go get it done. They didn't give the sales guys a roadmap or instructions on how to do it. The salesmen just went out and made it happen.

V: You liked that independence?

SS: I don't know if it was the independence, money or lifestyle. All I knew is that being in an office all day started to feel like a prison.

V: Much like this place.

SS: Funny guy! The work seemed meaningless, especially when you spent all day pushing paper or answering e-mails. It just wasn't me. The cubicle felt like a cage.

V: Interesting analogy.

SS: Desmond Morris wrote a book called *The Human Zoo*. He discusses how being in buildings and cubicles is not natural, which is why many people have some type of mental disorder. In the book, he describes a tiger pacing neurotically back and forth in its cage. Morris concluded that the animal was suffering from some type of disorder brought on by his caged environment. When I read that, I knew what he meant; I knew what the tiger felt like, pacing back and forth in my cubicle. If I didn't get out, I didn't know how much longer I could stand it.

V: So going on sales calls with salesmen alleviated some of that constriction.

SS: Oh, you don't know the half of it. Being able to travel was liberating. Exhilarating. You're flying to new states, new cities, even new countries. I enjoyed traveling with the salespeople on sales calls. I liked the fact that the sale hinged on my ability to deliver a flawless presentation from the front of the room.

V: Most people would buckle or fold under that type of pressure. Why didn't you?

SS: I can't say. All I knew is that, having learned how to give great presentations, I was halfway there to being in sales. All I needed was a break.

V: You place a great deal of emphasis on presenting.

SS: If you can't communicate and sell your ideas or concepts from the front of the room, you'll never make it in sales. Everything is about presenting. When you put an offer in a client's hands, you have to present it correctly. If you're greeting a customer for the first time, you have to present yourself correctly. I don't know who said, "All the world is a stage," but in the business of selling, "All the world is presenting."

*Transcript Note > Interviewee talks about
when he knew he wanted to be in sales.
Profit motive played a strong role.*

V: When did you know for sure, with 100%
certainty, that you wanted to be in sales?

SS: I was with a salesman by the name of
Ken. If I recall correctly, we flew out to
Iowa to do a presentation to this company's
the board of directors, who made the final
decision. We were one of three companies
presenting in this final round of a major
bid. They started out with ten companies;
it was now down to the final three. Winner
takes all, and the stakes were high. How
high? Five million dollars for this one
project. We also knew there would be add-on
work down the road, so the potential could
be as little as ten million and maybe as
high as fifteen million. Ken was feeling
the pressure because his numbers hadn't
been great up to that point, and the year
was half over. For Ken, we were in the
seventh inning and he needed a home run,
bad!

V: So what happened?

SS: What do you think happened, Einstein?
We won the bid! The presentation was not
only flawless, we had more information than
they ever expected to get. We cleaned the
other two companies' clocks.

V: Ken must've been happy.

SS: There's the understatement of the day
so far. When Ken got the news, he was
ecstatic. He called our top management to
tell them we had beaten our toughest
competitors. It was not only a great win

financially for the company, it was a morale booster for everybody.

V: Did Ken ever thank you?

SS: Ken called me at the end of the day to thank me. A week later he stopped by the office to take me out to lunch to celebrate. I come to find out during the lunch break that his commission for the deal would be somewhere in the neighborhood of $50,000 when the final system was delivered and installed. When I heard that, I went numb. I didn't let Ken notice.

V: I take it that was the watershed moment for you to jump into sales?

SS: Fuckin' right. Ken didn't know shit about the products. Every time the customer asked a tough question, Ken would look at me to answer it. Ken was a typical catalog opener. This guy only knew the basics and didn't have a clue how they worked or functioned. So I'm thinking to myself, this is bullshit. I was the guy who spent late nights doing the design analysis for the system. I was the guy crunching numbers and redesigning to keep the system within the customer's budget, so we didn't price ourselves out of the race. I did all the legwork, and what do I get for my troubles? A lunch. A fuckin' lunch that set him back maybe twenty-five dollars. And this no-nothing, technically challenged, ill-equipped-to-present son of a bitch gets a $50,000 commission check! So, you ask, was that a watershed moment for me? You're fuckin' right it was!

V: Did you have any idea how much commissions were involved before that?

SS: No, I never really asked or even thought about it. Salespeople are very tightlipped about how much they make. They know if others find out, they'll get just as pissed as I did.

V: Why do you think Ken told you?

SS: I think the fucker was so giddy that he made some money and wasn't going to get fired that he just had to share. Or, my second theory is that once his wife found out he was getting that money, she gave him the best roll in the sack that he's had in years. Ha! Whatever it was, the bird sang that day at lunch, and I encouraged him to do so. I learned a lot that day about how much salespeople can make and the lifestyle they can have. I was hooked.

Transcript Note > Interviewee talks about the importance of letting others know what you want in order to move ahead.

V: So when did you finally move into sales?

SS: About six months or so after the lunch, a sales position became open. From the day I had lunch with Ken, I began dropping hints in the right places that I'd consider moving into sales.

V: What do you mean dropping hints? Where?

SS: One thing I learned early about moving around in a company: shyness will never get you anywhere. You have to let people in company – the right people, in positions of influence – you need to let people know your intentions and what you want your next move to be. If you don't, they'll never know and you'll never be considered.

V: In other words, you have to let people know what you want in order to get it.

SS: Absolutely. So many people in business today are frustrated with their jobs. If you ask them why, they'll tell you they hate their position inside the company. I ask them what they'd rather be doing, and they're more than happy to share with me. I ask them if they've shared their wishes with their boss or people who have the ability to make it happen, and their answer is? Nine times out ten, they'll say no. Ask them why they haven't, and they come up with a bunch of reasons: it's not the right time, if they really wanted me they would ask, I don't know if my boss would approve, and so on.

V: I see.

SS: My favorite excuse is this one: "If I ask, they'll think I'm not happy working for the company. Next thing you know I won't have a job." What a load of crap! These idiots are in denial. They ARE unhappy with their jobs, that's the point of asking for another position or promotion. The irony here is they're afraid to lose their job, when in reality what they're really losing is their life. What kind of existence is that?

V: Have you ever been in that situation?

SS: Oh yeah! It is scary; you're afraid to move. But what's scarier is the possibility of nothing ever changing. I've learned you have to ask. You have to ask. You can't be bashful in business. You have to be direct with people and tell them exactly what you want. These same people who are scared would be amazed at how much their life would change if they just took the time to ask or, at a minimum, express an interest in moving. In all aspects of life, we have to let people know what we want. We have to learn not to sit back silently and hope someone can read our mind. We have to ask!

V: So, back to dropping hints.

SS: So what I did was let people in the sales management team know I would be interested in a sales position. I let salespeople I traveled with know I was interested. Surprisingly, they were very supportive and asked me what they could do to help. I simply asked them to let their managers know I was interested. I let anyone related to sales know I was interested. So when a position became available, I was asked to interview. I had one great advantage over the other

34

candidate: my technical skills. I knew our products better than most salespeople, and the manager was ecstatic to have someone on the sales team with in-depth knowledge of the product. There's one thing that will always guarantee you a leg up on an interview: knowing the product.

V: So they hired you? Your campaigning worked?

SS: Yes, they did, and yes, it did. I was excited for the first time in a long time, and I was also nervous.

V: Nervous?

SS: Well, sales is one of those professions where your contribution and your performance are easy to measure. No longer was I working as part of a team; this time I was standing alone with a quota. I had never carried a quota before, and in sales that's the only measuring stick that counts.

V: 'Quota' being your sales number for the year?

SS: Yes. It's a go/no-go, pass/fail type of sales metric. You either make your quota or you don't. That absoluteness scared me. There's no place to hide when you don't hit your sales number.

Transcript Note > Interviewee discusses how a mentor helped accelerate his sales career.

V: How did you handle the pressure of starting out for the first time on your own?

SS: I had a guardian angel.

V: What?

SS: Just kidding. I didn't have a guardian angel, but he could've been one. The manager that I went to work for was a guy named Jose Santana. Jose had a reputation of being one of the best, if not the best salesperson the company had ever had. He had been with the company almost ten years, and he knew all the tricks of the trade and all the places not to step. Jose was kind enough to take me under his wing. I loved that man! I don't know if he knows it, but he's the greatest in my book and still is to this day.

V: So Jose was a mentor of sorts?

SS: Jose was a pro. I had the pleasure of traveling with him on many occasions before I ventured off on my own. I remember watching everything he did closely. How he greeted people, how he socialized, how he presented, how he sold the company's products without overselling. During dinner meetings with clients, I'd watch how he masterfully controlled the conversations. He was great at mixing business with pleasure. He enjoyed entertaining customers and making them feel like long-lost friends. This was an exciting time for me. Even though I was part of the sales team, Jose made me feel like a kid going to the circus for the first time; I watched in amazement when he performed. Jose was the show. The guy could charm the pants off anyone. I knew right there and then the type of salesman I wanted to be. I modeled a lot of my style and approach to business much like Jose did.

V: Sounds like you lucked out the first time.

SS: I think the best break a first time salesperson can get is to be mentored and tutored by the best in the business. I was lucky, and I knew it. I've seen other new upstarts get no guidance. Over time they flounder and eventually fail, leaving the sales profession altogether. In some cases they should've never been in sales, but in many cases they just didn't have the guidance of a good mentor or a supportive environment.

V: Aside from your friend Jose, are there any others who helped you in your sales career?

SS: No one more than Jose in terms of the mechanics of what to do in front of a customer. When I traveled with him, it was the best LIVE training you could possibly ask for.

V: Do you study other salespeople?

SS: I do and always will. I love when a salesman tries to sell me when I'm in the consumer seat. I learn from watching how others do it.

V: Give me an example.

SS: I remember pulling into a gas station one evening. As I approached the counter to pay for the gas, I heard a young man behind me say, "Nice car, mister." I turned around and saw him sitting on a crate. He couldn't have been more than 13 or so years old. I said, "Thank you." He responded, "Looks like you take real good care of your car." I said, "I do my best." The kid made me feel good about my car, and then he lowered the sales boom on me. "Mister, would you like to buy some candies I'm selling for my organization. We're trying to raise money for a trip." Before I knew it, I was forking over ten bucks to the kid for some bars of chocolate from under the crate. I mean, how could I say no to this kid who just gave me a great compliment and made me feel good about myself? As I drove away, I remember thinking, "Damn, I just got sold."

V: Were you mad?

SS: Hell, no! I started to laugh. All I remember thinking is, "That kid's gonna make one helluva salesman when he grows up!"

V: Aside from personal experiences, do you study or read about the business of sales?

SS: Absolutely. There are a lot of great authors and trainers out there who know the real deal when it comes to selling. I have a disdain for those who sell canned sales training programs that are more theory than reality-oriented.

V: If you had to pick one person, aside from your mentor, whom you admire as a salesperson, who would that be?

SS: That's a tough question. But if I had to choose an author or trainer out there today, it would be a gentleman by the name of Zig Ziglar.

V: I've heard of him.

SS: If you hadn't, I'd be worried. I like his training style and the way he weaves a good sales story. He's learned and lives by the sales axiom "Stories sell, facts tell."

V: How about the best sales book you've ever read?

SS: Damn it, man, you're asking a lot here.

V: Come on, narrow it down to one.

SS: I can't pick one. But I will tell you about the first sales book I read that made an impact on me.

V: Fair enough.

SS: One day I was sifting through books for sale, and I came across a book called *SPIN Selling* by Neil Rackham. I bought it, went home and started reading right away.

V: Why did this book stand out?

SS: It's one of those books you have to continuously put down, because it has such great content, you want to take it in by stopping and reflecting on the major points being made. The book not only breaks down the sales process into four basic phases, but it uses real world questioning and probing techniques that can be used to sell into any industry. But more important, it's based on real world testimonies and tests done in the field, not by some PhD.

V: I have a PhD.

SS: Sorry, no offense.

V: Just kidding, I don't have one.

SS: Cute.

V: Let me ask an obvious question: do you think it's important to stay on top of your sales game by continuing to read and learn about sales?

SS: Without a doubt. If you're serious about sales, you have to read and study constantly.

V: What do you suggest?

SS: If you can read one sales book a month, I think you're ahead of the game.

V: Don't you find a lot of these books repetitive? I read some sales books before coming here and found that many of them blur into one another. The content is too similar – little or no difference.

SS: It's hard to find a good sales book these days. Many books today are a regurgitation of basic sales strategies. But, like anything else, if you dig deep enough you'll always find a good book. And if you can glean at least one or two ideas from it, ask yourself how much money will that one idea make you.

V: You've talked about personal training and education; let's talk about training from a company standpoint.

Transcript Note > Interviewee begins to discuss the effects of training on sales success.

V: You mentioned earlier that salespeople need a good, supportive environment to grow. Were you referring to a company's training program?

SS: Aw, man, it kills me at times. Companies spend millions on promotional campaigns, product development, research, and all that. But when it comes to putting together a training program for their front-line salespeople, these companies fall short.

V: Would you say that's the norm?

SS: Based on my experience, definitely yes. I know there are companies out there who underestimate the value of training, and most companies don't put together a solid training program. Now, when I say training program I'm not talking about "Let's get together once or twice a year and discuss the new products." I mean real training programs that show salespeople how to sell and not tell.

V: That's an interesting phrase.

SS: What, "sell, not tell?" There's a huge difference. The untrained person will tell the customer about his or her new products. Trained salespeople sell the product by showing customers how they can save money or be better off using the product.

V: Maybe companies think training programs cost too much to create and maintain.

SS: That's short-term thinking. They're asking the wrong question.

V: What do you mean?

SS: Management, after spending hundreds of thousands or millions on a product, will ask, "How much is it going to cost us to develop a training program?" When the real question should be, "How much is it going to cost us if we don't? How much revenue will we lose if our salespeople aren't adequately trained?" These questions go unanswered or worst yet, never asked at all. You can't put a value on a training program, and most companies literally don't get it. They'll go out and hire the top salespeople in the business and put together lucrative packages for them. Once hired, they tell the salesperson the equivalent of "Now, go sell." And when they fail, they blame themselves for hiring the wrong person - never questioning that maybe they failed the salesperson by not providing adequate training. It boggles the fucking mind how short-sighted these corporate heads are. Maybe one day they'll get their heads out of their asses. Maybe they'll get it one day.

V: In their defense, they may say that training is the salesperson's responsibility.

SS: That's like a mother saying, "Okay, I gave birth to you, now it's your job to make it in this world." These companies that don't provide support are setting these salespeople up for failure, pure and simple. Every product or service requires a sales strategy if it's going to succeed. Instead of spending hundreds of hours in strategic meetings discussing what should be done, spend a tenth of that putting together a strong tactical strategy.

V: You mentioned both 'strategy' and 'tactical' in the same sentence.

SS: Huge difference. Most companies assign 80% of their time and effort to the strategic part of the business and 20% to the tactical side.

V: I think I understand the difference, but run it by me from your perspective.

SS: Strategy is all about planning how to attack a market. Tactics are the day-to-day activities needed to carry out the strategy. In my opinion, we should spend more time on tactics, less on strategy. Too often, management goes into a 'paralysis by analysis' by refining their strategies constantly. So much so that they dedicate little time to the day-to-day, week-to-week, or month-to-month tactics needed to reach their revenue goals.

V: But shouldn't the salespeople, not management, be concerned with the tactics of selling?

SS: That's like saying soldiers are responsible not only for the fighting, but they have to find the tools and weapons as well. What I'm saying is that many salespeople walk onto the field armed with a flimsy brochure and some pretty business cards. That's not preparing them to sell; that's setting them up to fail.

V: Got it.

Transcript Note > Interviewee talks about how creativity and dishonesty play a part in sales success.

V: I'd like to shift to another topic.

SS: Go ahead.

V: I'd like to know if creativity had anything to do with your success in sales.

SS: Creativity?

V: Yeah, you know, did you think outside the box? Did you approach sales differently than others?

SS: I don't know if I would categorize it as solely creativity. I think there's creativity and then there's hustling.

V: Hustling?

SS: Yeah, you know, where you outsmart the other guy before he knows what hit him.

V: I think I know what you mean. You have to be creative to out-hustle the other guy, am I right?

SS: Yes and no. Creativity is out-thinking the other person. Hustling is out-smarting the other person by doing what others won't do.

V: I see them as one and the same. Help me out. Give me an example of both and maybe I'll understand better.

SS: Maybe you're right. You be the judge. Do you remember back in the day when junk yards would pay you for metal beer cans and Coke cans?

V: That's going back, but yes.

SS: One day my friend Nano and I were out collecting cans, trying to generate some money to buy candy and comic books.

V: Out of curiosity, what comic books did you read?

SS: Just about anything. *Archie*, *Richie Rich*, *Casper*, *Tales of the Unexpected*, *Rawhide*, *The Justice League*, *Thor the Thunder God*, *Superman*, *Spiderman*, *Fantastic Four*, *Aquaman*, a whole bunch of others. Mr. Mitchell would always put the new comic books on display in his windows. I still remember gawking through the window, planning which comic books I would buy next. I had boxes of them.

V: Do you still have them?

SS: Nah! Somewhere between being a kid and puberty, the comics were lost. I can only imagine what they'd go for today in the open market.

V: I'm sure it would be a pretty penny. But get back to the cans.

SS: Okay. Me and Nano got a couple of bags and went out collecting cans wherever we could find them. Back then, there were a lot of vacant lots and people would litter in the neighborhood. Today we take those corner garbage cans for granted. Back in the day, the street was the garbage can. So Nano and I really tore a hole in our shoes trying to collect enough cans to buy some comic books. Junkyards would give you something like 5 cents per pound of metal. That's a lot of can collecting to get comic books that cost 25 to 50 cents. Once we got the first load collected, we went to the junkyard and walked away with about 20 cents, I believe. We were destroyed. All that work, hours of gathering, collecting and smashing them down for a measly 20 cents. Not enough to buy one comic book. What made the day worse was that it was raining and all the lots we explored were muddy. Our shoes looked like crap!

V: Ouch!

SS: Ouch is right. We were determined to get those comic books, but we were finding fewer and fewer cans as the day went on. Remember, we were on foot, so our geographical coverage wasn't large. I remember bringing back a load to my house and thinking we only had about 10 cents worth of cans. Then, like a bolt of lightning, I got this great idea. Since all the cans had to be smashed, I suggested we put mud in the cans before we smash them. Once smashed, the excess mud would ooze out, but some would stay in the cans and make the cans heavier.

V: Ahhhh! I see where you're going.

SS: Damn right. Since the cans were heavier, we collected less cans but made more money. The idiots at the junkyard never caught on. We were happy as shit when we both got our favorite comic books at the end of the day!

V: Congratulations on your dishonesty.

SS: Dishonesty? I like to think of it as being innovative and creative.

V: Call it what you want, it was dishonest anyway you cut it.

SS: You may be right, but it worked.

V: So do the ends justify the means?

SS: I knew that fucking question was coming from the indignant tone in your voice. Look, I was young and dumb. Excuse me for applying some creativity to an otherwise shitty job. Keep in mind I was also beautifying our neighborhood in the process. So there was some redeeming value in our dishonesty.

V: Nice try. Will you admit you were wrong?

SS: (pause) Yes, I admit what I did was wrong. And I can say with 100% certainty that since that day I've not put mud in any client's shipment or applied my thumb on any scale to increase the weight. You happy?

V: As long as you admit that what you did was wrong, that's all that matters.

SS: Can you at least give me some creativity points for my age?

V: No. If creativity is applied ethically, then I'll concede that to you, but not in this case. You were wrong then, and if you did that today, you'd wind up in jail like those CEOs who ravaged their companies with 'creative' accounting.

SS: Hmm, padded cell or six-by-eight cinderblock cell. Which one gets better food?

V: Very funny! Do you like to take advantage of other people if you can?

SS: What business do you have passing judgment on me and condemning me!

V: I'm not judging, I'm trying to understand you. I'm just asking a simple question. If you could take advantage of a situation by applying some 'creativity' as you did with the cans, knowing it would hurt someone else, would you do it today?

SS: No, I wouldn't. I've learned there are no shortcuts when it comes to making money and success. I took a shortcut with my cans, but sooner or later if I had kept doing it, I'm sure they would've figured it out. I lucked out that they didn't.

V: What do you think of people who get away with taking shortcuts?

SS: I used to get mad. Real mad. I've been in sales situations where someone put 'mud' in my proposal and gave it no chance of winning. I know now that there are people worth doing business with and others that we should just avoid.

V: In your sales career, have you met people who used creative methods to cheat the system?

SS: Oh yeah! You'd be amazed at how much of that goes on. I've reached a point in my life where I can't live that way. I know I can cheat the system, but I refuse to do so. In the past, I've paid the price in the short term for not doing it the right way; now at least I sleep better at night doing it the right way.

V: Have you ever cheated the system?

SS: I don't know if I call it 'cheating the system.' I'd like to think that I shortcut the system - big difference. Now before your imagination runs away with you, it's nothing as bad as you might think. If I were brought up in front of a judge in a court of law, the most it would warrant is a harsh reprimand or a slap on the wrist.

V: So you've bent the rules?

SS: Yeah, that's more like it. We salespeople are like children at times. We like to see how much we can get away with before being scolded by upper management.

V: So nothing too serious?

SS: Not really. Compared to some of the stuff we see in the news today with corporative executives, what I did was child's play.

V: Have you ever met anyone who shortcut the system so much that they actually damaged the company's reputation or put shareholders at risk?

SS: Many years ago there was a company that, in order to meet their quarterly projections and not suffer a drop in their stock prices, would actually ship out empty boxes or, in some cases, a box with only the shell of the product inside.

V: You lost me there.

SS: Let's say you were manufacturing computers. And let's assume the company was expected to ship X amount by the end of the quarter. If the numbers looked like they were going to fall short, and production couldn't deliver enough products to ship, instructions were given to ship the computers without anything inside them – just the chassis.

V: But customers would know it was only a chassis once they received it.

SS: Naïve bastard, listen closely and you could learn something. Yes, the customer would receive the product, realize it was defective and call the company. The company would *mea culpa*. "Oh, we're so sorry, there must've been a mix-up in production, we deeply apologize." But by then, it wouldn't matter. The company would claim it met its X amount of shipment, its revenue target number, and take no hit to its stock price.

V: What about the return goods? The empty boxes?

SS: Well, the company would take the product back and try to ship out a new one as soon as possible. Either way, the order was fulfilled from an accounting standpoint and the revenue was counted in the previous quarter. Get it?

V: Yeah, I get it. That's crooked as hell.

SS: It's like me putting mud in the cans. The only thing is that I know the difference between being a kid fooling the guy at the junkyard with loaded Coke cans, and seriously violating shareholder trust as an adult. As I got older, I put my childhood ways behind me; others apparently haven't. I'm not condemning business as a whole, just letting you know what I saw.

V: So along the way you grew up?

SS: You're an asshole for someone so smart. There is such as thing as being too creative!

V: Just kidding. Okay, you've shown me what type of trouble too much creativity can cause. What about hustling?

SS: Hustling is a matter of working harder and smarter. Going the extra mile in any profession is what gets most people in the top 5-10 percent of those who make great money. But there's no point in going the extra mile if you're not smart enough to know which way to go. Constantly out-thinking and out-working your competitor will put you in the number one spot.

*Transcript Note > Interviewee discusses
product knowledge and its impact on sales.*

V: I'm inclined to agree with you, but can
you still out-hustle the other guy if your
product is not the best?

SS: Are you baiting me?

V: I don't understand.

SS: You're trying to get me to say that
only the salesperson with the best product
wins the deal?

V: That's one way of putting it.

SS: Such a diplomatic answer. We were doing
so well up until now. Do you or do you not
believe that the best product always wins
out?

V: I don't believe so.

SS: Yes or no, you shit?

V: Um, yes.

SS: (Makes a harsh buzzer sound) Ehhhh!
Wrong answer. The best product doesn't
always win out. The best salesman with the
best product presentation and the best
product match will win out.

V: Ah! So you have to have the best product
match!

SS: You're not listening. I gave you three
components to a successful sale; did you
get it?

V: Yes, a good salesperson, presentation
and best match or fit for the company.

SS: Let's put the first two aside and focus on the best match for the company. It is rare, I mean rare, that a company will find an exact product match in the market for their needs. One reason is that customers have so many varying needs that the product would have to be developed in-house just for them. Second, customers don't know what they want in many cases because they haven't been shown what they need.

V: You lost me on the second part.

SS: Once a customer starts using a product, invariably, new wants or needs will develop.

V: I'm confused.

SS: You asked me if the best product always wins out. I told you no. Why? Because in many cases, even the customer doesn't know what they want beyond the immediate future. A salesperson's job is to help guide the customer through the labyrinth of product features and benefits so that they come to the obvious conclusion that they have to buy from you. The means to accomplish this is a well-prepared presentation. So my point is this: the product that will win is the one that is presented in the best light by the best salesperson, but isn't necessarily the best match at the time. Does that answer your question?

V: Very much so. But what if a salesperson doesn't know his product or how to pull off such a presentation, what then?

SS: Then the company is screwed!

V: Is the salesperson screwed also?

SS: That's a foregone conclusion. The bigger concern is the company that must suffer the slings and arrows of poor sales, not because of poor product but due to poor training. The real cost to the company is incalculable.

V: Is it really the company's obligation to train the salesperson? Shouldn't the salesperson take on that responsibility?

SS: Now you're starting to ask great questions.

V: I am overjoyed that you approve.

SS: Man, you're a piece of work. Did your mama stop breastfeeding you too early?

V: Answer the question.

SS: A company's responsibility is to provide the tools to make selling easier. Any company that doesn't take the time to develop a good product or service training program is handicapping themselves.

V: So it is a company's responsibility?

SS: Listen to what I'm saying. It's the company's responsibility to provide the tools to make selling easier. It's the salesman's responsibility to use those tools.

V: Yes, but what if the company doesn't provide the necessary tools? What is the salesman's responsibility then?

SS: Well, he has two choices. Find another company with a better training program as he blindly struggles to sell his existing product. Or take the initiative to learn as much as he can about the product. It doesn't speak well of a company that doesn't have the right tools to help sell the product.

V: What's been your experience?

SS: They come in all shades. Some companies have outstanding training programs and people dedicated to developing and enhancing salespeople whether they're just beginning or experienced. Other companies are just plain lazy. They have maybe one annual training session a year where people fly in to learn as much as they can in one day.

V: Maybe some companies can't afford to train everybody they way they should be trained.

SS: And maybe the moon is made of cheese. Companies add up the cost of developing a training program and conclude that it's too expensive, but fail to add up the intangible cost of a poorly-trained sales force and the gradual erosion their ineptitude has on their sales numbers.

V: What about the salespeople? What responsibility do they have?

SS: If the company provides training information and they don't use it, they're idiots. I personally took responsibility for learning my products no matter how little or scattered the information was. If need be, I'd call the home office and ask to speak directly with the developers who knew the product or service we offered intimately. There's no excuse for not knowing, given today's technology.

V: By that you mean ...?

SS: All of it: cell phones, computers, e-mail, the Internet. All the information we need is just a few keystrokes away. And yet, I've seen it happen. I've met salespeople who've been in the company for more than a year and are still clueless about their own products or services. It's like they're waiting to learn by osmosis or something. I never got it and to this day still don't get how people can go around selling what they don't understand.

V: How do they sell?

SS: If you want to call it selling. I call it dumbass luck. One of my favorite sayings is that even a blind squirrel eventually finds a nut. Some of these guys get lucky and land some large account and milk that cash cow dry. Others are simply account managers or catalog openers who are ordered to babysit large accounts.

V: Isn't an account manager a salesperson?

SS: Many account managers today are assigned an account, a specific client, to babysit. In some cases, all this requires is that you be there to blow the customer's nose when they sneeze and wipe their ass when needed. No real selling is going on. It's just account babysitting.

V: Are all account managers 'babysitters?'

SS: Not all. There are what I call the purest. This is a breed of account managers who know they have a good client and always work on trying to sell the customer more instead of just filling orders. They're pros when it comes to fattening the cash cow by finding ways to sell them more and more. These sales types are a far cry from catalog openers.

V: What are catalog openers?

SS: Lazy bastards. All they want is the paycheck and the sales lifestyle. They don't know shit about the product. God forbid a customer asks an intelligent question. Their favorite line is, "I don't know, but let me get back to you." They never study the products or even care about what's new. They learn enough to give the illusion of knowing, but they don't.

V: I can see there's no love lost here.

SS: Catalog openers should be taken out to the back and shot. They're parasites who are too lazy to do their job, but love the paycheck. It irked me when a salesperson was given an account to manage that required little or no effort while the rest of us were busting our asses trying to get a sale. To add insult to injury, these lazy asswipes were given awards at the annual sales meeting for their great 'salesmanship.'

V: You've seen that happen?

SS: Brother, you have no idea how many catalog openers I've met who got rewarded for shit they had no hand in. Used to turn my stomach.

V: That bad?

SS: So bad that I finally had to learn to mentally block them out. It was sad when real salespeople with a sincere interest in helping the company grow were given little or no recognition because they were handed dead accounts. Let's just say that when it comes to sales compensation, not everyone gets what they deserve. We'll leave it at that.

V: Fine with me. Let's get back to the other component of a sale, the presentation.

SS: The toughest part is getting to the point of doing a presentation for the customer.

V: Okay, we'll take a step back. Before we talk about how you prepare and deliver a presentation, explain to me how you get the appointment in the first place, if it's a new client. In fact, how do you decide which clients to go after?

Transcript Note > Interviewee discusses territory assignment as it relates to sales success.

SS: You need to take another step back and start with your territory and who your customers are, and then we can talk about getting on the inside.

V: Alright, let's start there.

SS: Sales success depends a great deal on the customer or territory you're given. I remember while working for a high tech company, a few of the salespeople got the cream of the crop customers while the rest of us begged for business.

V: Who made the decision as to which salespeople got which customers?

SS: Usually management. The vice president or director of sales. They were usually under a lot of pressure to meet their sales quota. So I guess I understood their motivation to put the best sales manager on the best sales account.

V: You mean, you weren't the best?

SS: Look, if my hands were loose right now, I'd put them around your friggin' neck. When I first started in sales, yes, I wasn't the best. I thought I was, but what arrogant shit doesn't think he's the best when he first starts out?

V: Looking back, is there anything you would've done differently?

SS: Yeah, back then I thought I knew it all. I thought I should've gotten the major accounts. I hated those management pricks for always giving someone else the better accounts. Time has given me the privilege of perspective, and after being chained in this room for quite some time now, I have a great deal of perspective.

V: Share some.

SS: Well. (pause) I don't know where to begin. I understand now that I didn't know as much as I thought I knew when I was younger. I wish I would've redirected all that anger at management and other salespeople down a more positive avenue.

V: So you were an angry young salesman?

SS: Cut it out with the psychobabble. I admit I was angry at times.

V: Who was the anger directed at mostly?

SS: I already told you how much I hated salespeople who got away with doing as little as possible and still made the big bucks. I've met too many salespeople who learned the art of kissing ass and getting the sweet customers.

V: Have you ever 'kissed ass,' as you so eloquently put it?

SS: Go fuck yourself!

V: It's a fair question!

SS: Look, we all have to kiss ass at one time or another. We all have to take orders shoved down our throats and pretend that we like them. I'd like to tell you I never kissed ass but that would be a big-ass lie. I've patronized my superiors. I've flattered them with compliments when appropriate.

V: So you have kissed ass?

SS: And you haven't? You've never had to purse your lips in agreement when you knew the decision to do something was wrong? C'mon. Don't bullshit me. We all have to eat shit once in a while, and we all have to pucker once in a while.

V: Then why are you so mad at people who suck up?

SS: There're people who will pretend to go along for one reason or another. They'll agree to things because the pressure to do otherwise would be too great. But there's another breed of humanoid who has taken ass kissing to an art form. Their sole motive is to flatter the hell out of their superiors no matter how undignified it may be.

V: So you're telling me there is a point beyond which you will not kiss ass?

SS: Fuckin' right! I believe it was Clint Eastwood who said, "A man's got to know his limitations." And, amigo, I knew mine. There is a point beyond which no amount of money, rewards or accolades would cause me to pucker up and kiss ass.

V: What is that point?

SS: If at any time I had to compromise my integrity, where the difference between right and wrong was black and white, I'd sooner get fired than do it.

V: So you have a moral code.

SS: Call it what you want, there is no way I'm selling my soul to the corporate devil just to make a buck. Others seem to do it with ease; I couldn't. Never will.

V: How did you manage to be successful as a salesman if you didn't play the game?

SS: I never said I didn't play the game. I said I never sold my soul playing the game. Whether people want to admit it or not, it really does matter that other people like you if you want to move up in any organization.

V: How did you get people to like you?

SS: Different ways, depending on the circumstances. Each situation had its own unique rules for behavior and comportment.

V: You mean you would adapt to a given situation? You would compromise?

SS: No. You're missing the point. Let me give you an example. One company I worked for had a certain corporate culture, and I couldn't work my way in. You know what I mean?

V: Yeah, I think so. You couldn't fit into the group. You couldn't find a space where you belonged.

SS: Hmm, yeah, something like that. No matter how hard I worked to prove that I was competent, I still felt like an outsider. You know you're an outsider when you've been there a few months and no one asks you to join their group for lunch. I didn't get it. I started to feel a little resentful. But I kept my wits about me, and I was determined to find a way to fit. The funny thing, the answer was right in front of me all the time. These folks really like to go golfing. So I decided to take up golfing. Now, being from the inner city and raised poor, the only golf course I saw was on television.

V: So how did you learn?

SS: I went to the local public golf course. It was a 9-hole, par-3 golf course and they offered a six-week clinic – once-a-week lessons for beginners. I signed up. They gave me some sticks to start out with. As I progressed, I went out and got my first set of golf clubs. That was a great day.

V: And the impact at work?

SS: At first it was slow. I would come into work and strike up a conversation about business and drop a hint or two that I was taking golf lessons. As the weeks progressed, I asked more questions about the game. After a while I found myself having lengthy conversations at the cafeteria or in the manager's office about tips and tricks to improve my golf game. Then, one day it happened. I was invited to go out golfing with a few of the managers. I reminded them that I still sucked at it. That didn't seem to faze them. One guy actually said, "Great, you'll at least make me look good." Ha! So off I went.

V: So things got better at work?

SS: Much more than that, actually. Once you're on the golf course with people, they seem to loosen up and be freer with their information and insight on what's going on with the company. I quickly realized, like many have, that socializing outside of work is great way to gather information about changes that might be coming.

V: You mean the managers just spilled their guts?

SS: Not exactly. Over time, a trust and a bond begins to build. This taught me a very valuable lesson about working relationships and how decisions are often made based on who you like to be around.

V: So being liked helped your sales career?

SS: There's that understatement again. Being liked helps, period! Learning to adjust or, better yet, acculturate is a big part of success in any company.

V: Acculturate?

SS: You know, blending into the corporate culture without losing your identity.

V: I know what it is; I just find it odd that a salesman would use the term.

SS: All salespeople aren't dumb. We actually do read things other than brochures and manuals.

V: Got it. My bad.

SS: When I think about learning the game of golf just to fit in, I don't feel as though I compromised. What is the saying – "When in Rome, do as the Romans do." In business you have to be flexible in your outlook to see things from someone else's perspective.

V: Isn't that a good sales trait in general?

SS: Absolutely!

V: Out of curiosity, do you still play golf?

SS: No, not as much. The next company I went to didn't have a golf mentality.

V: Do you still have the clubs?

SS: You betcha. I call them my six-figure sticks.

V: Because they helped you earn a six-figure salary?

SS: Bet your ass they did. That's the best return on investment I've ever made. And before I forget to mention it, it's important to point out the obvious. As salespeople, we are taught that people buy from people they like. Yes?

V: Yes.

SS: Well, here's another news flash: managers promote people they like. People in positions of power want to surround themselves with not only competent people, but people they like and can relate to. At a minimum, managers will give you some consideration when it comes to assigning you a territory, an account or even a sales quota, if you're competent and they like you.

V: Question: Did you change, personally, when you went out golfing? I mean, did you have to alter who you were to fit in?

SS: Yes and no. On the course, these guys were all business. They're competitive beasts who want to dominate the golf course. So when we played golf, there was some idle chitchat, but my focus and theirs was always beating the course. So yes, I was more restrained on the course. But afterwards, we'd stop at the pub and get a few beers and tell our 18-hole war stories about the putt that got away, or the magnificent drive that almost was, if it weren't for the lake being two feet beyond your drive. At that moment, you went back to the real you. I think people want to see the real you. They measure their level of trust by observing you to see how genuine you really are. I've seen many fakers try to be 'politicos' on the course and after; it never worked. They were never invited back if someone sensed they were working the angles on the golf course. Does that answer your question?

V: It does. But how do you know how much you should expose yourself? In other words, how do you know when you're being too genuine?

SS: Ha! That sounds like an oxymoron, 'being too genuine.'

V: You know what I mean. How do you know how comfortable you can get around others?

SS: Use your powers of observation; the clues are always right in front of you. You have to adapt to the human terrain. Here are two extreme examples to illustrate my point. When I go out golfing with a group of Mormons, which I have by the way, I take note that they don't drink or smoke and, more often than not, they don't even swear. Knowing this, I'm the guy that will order a Coca Cola with a twist of lemon and suck on a lollipop between holes, and suppress any urge to swear by using surrogates like 'darn' or 'flippin'' or 'horse manure' when I would shank the ball or miss a putt. Now, if I'm with your stereotypical salesmen where drinks between holes are allowed and a Dominican cigar is part of the facial décor, then I adapt. And yes, if cursing is going on, I unleash my share – but never outdoing my golf mates. It's all about adopting their modalities for the moment.

V: Some would call that selling out.

SS: I would say to those some, again, to kiss my ass. It's not personal, it's business. If someone wants to 'be themselves' at all times, then by all means do it. Experience has taught me that these people will alienate themselves. Imagine a Mormon golfer going with a rowdy, hard drinking, cigar chain-smoking gang of three golfing. At the end of the day, someone is going to feel out of place. Either the three will feel uncomfortable having the other guy there, or vice versa. And when you make others feel uncomfortable, I will guarantee you, you won't be invited again. I'm not selling out, I'm buying in.

V: What's the poor Mormon to do if everyone in the company feels that way?

SS: Find another company or find a way to coexist within the culture without compromising his or her integrity. Not an easy task if the two cultures are diametrically opposed.

V: Does that mean he won't get promoted?

SS: No. I didn't say that. But he will have a harder time; that's not my opinion, that's human nature in business. I could be wrong, but I've seen it too often to doubt it exists.

V: Alright, back to relationships. Establishing good relationships within the company – did they really help you get better territory or customers?

SS: Yes. Look, I can recall many times when who would work where was discussed over a cold beer. There was no master planning; it was discussed, and then it was done. I've also seen careers teeter on the edge of termination simply by a few statements made during casual, after-work conversations. I'm a firm believer that more deals are consummated and careers made or ruined after 5 pm.

V: Wow! That's a harsh reality. It almost sounds like hard work doesn't matter.

SS: You shit, don't put words into my mouth. Hard work counts. But you can't just sit back and hope someone notices your work. There's a book by Rick Page called *Hope is Not a Strategy*. Now, that guy knew what the real deal was. Nothing happens by chance; you have to make the chances happen. Success is about hard work, but you have to help success along when you work in a corporate pit.

V: Odd term, 'pit.' Why use the pit analogy? Freudian slip?

SS: You really are a piece of work, Sigmund.

V: I'm just saying, of all the analogies you could've chosen, why 'pit?'

SS: When I think of the word 'pit,' I think of Indiana Jones in *Raiders of the Lost Ark*. Or was it *Temple of Doom*? Doesn't matter. Remember when he was stuck in the pit with all those snakes? Each snake was waiting for him to make the wrong move and piss them off so they could bite him. Corporate America, especially in sales, you have people who can't wait to see you fail.

V: That's a fatalistic attitude.

SS: Call it what you want, but I've seen people cheer for someone's demise instead of cheering for their success.

V: So people in sales, in your own organization, can hinder your sales success if you're not careful.

SS: Not only those in sales, but those in the rest of the corporation will do the same thing.

V: Whoa! Wait a minute. There's no way that people in the office conspire against salespeople.

SS: 'Conspire' is too harsh of a word. Let's just say that if they have the chance, and you're not well-liked, they'd just as well throw you an anchor as a life preserver.

V: Well, you've got my attention now. Give me an example of what you mean, if you have one.

SS: Alright. Take that silver spoon out of your mouth and listen to this. When I worked for a large Fortune 500 corporation, we were on the verge of launching a new system that had literally cost hundreds of millions – *hundreds* of *millions* – to bring to market. If a salesman sold one system, that would make their quota for the year. But keep in mind that these systems required a long sales cycle.

V: What's a long sales cycle?

SS: A long sales cycle is common for expensive products. From start to finish, a deal can take three, six or twelve months to close. We refer to these deals as long sales cycle deals.

V: Got it.

SS: Now, due to its long sales cycle, the commission on the sale of these systems was incredible generous. It had to be, because if the salesperson lost the deal, that could mean zero dollars for the whole year. The commissions being earned by the top salespeople were so large that the accounting department started to get upset at the large paychecks they had to write to these top salesmen who closed a few deals that year. They then decided to lower the commission rate and, listen closely, put a cap, a limit, on how much they could make on sales.

V: And? What's wrong with that?

SS: Are you familiar with the concept of unintended consequences? You know, when things don't work out the way you planned and you wind up causing more harm than good?

V: Yeah.

SS: Well, these penny pinchers in accounting decided to make these compensation changes. By the way, it wasn't because the company was losing money that the changes were made. In fact, the company was making a hefty margin even after paying out commissions.

V: Then why did accounting want to change the sales compensation plans?

SS: Because they were a bunch of fucking envious idiots, that's why! Rumor had it they actually *congratulated* each other when the final compensation plan was approved by the vice president of sales, who himself had no balls and wasn't willing to stand up to the Chief Financial Officer whose final approval was needed.

V: But –

SS: Wait, there's more. When the new compensation plans were presented to the salespeople, they went ballistic. Many had been counting on those commissions to offset the lack of sales for other products. When the accounting folks heard about the salespeople's reaction, you know what they did?

V: What?

SS: Those friggin' bean counters actually celebrated like they had just pulled off the biggest commission coup in the history of sales. There's no better way to demoralize a sales force than reaching into their pockets and taking their money from them. And there is no better way to undermine your sales manager than for him to learn he couldn't stop it from happening. That day marked the beginning of end in terms of sales.

V: What do mean?

SS: When word got around that the commission plan was revamped to a fraction of what it was, and that a cap limit had been put in place, what do you think the natural reaction of salesmen would be?

V: Sell less?

SS: Sell less with a vengeance. Salespeople are driven by the carrot a corporation dangles in front of them. That carrot is money, which represents lifestyle and financial freedom. Take the carrot away, and the motivation is gone. With one pen stroke, the CFO and his horde of bean counters removed the carrot.

V: Yeah, but couldn't they still make money up to a point?

SS: Exactly, up to a point. When the new year began and the salesmen hit their quota for the new system – whereby they could make the most on commission – they stopped selling the new system any further. They moved off and started selling some of the smaller systems, because there was no maximum cap on those products. At the end of the year, the revenue numbers fell way short of expectation and management struggled to understand why until one of the senior execs learned of the cap. When he did, he was furious and immediately held a meeting to remove the cap. No heads rolled, but accounting was directed never to tamper with sales compensation again. As one executive reminded the CFO, "Accounting is a cost center, Sales is a profit center. Don't ever forget which group is paying the bills." Oh baby, I love that statement.

V: So the next year was better?

SS: Not really. The sales numbers were better but the damage had already been done. You have to understand, these were very expensive systems, and there weren't a lot of buyers who could afford them. When the salespeople stopped selling them the year prior, the competition had time to sneak in and cherry-pick the best customers. By the time the salespeople got back to selling these systems, it was too late in many cases. Remember, these systems had long sales cycles. It wasn't just a matter of dropping in to a customer's office and saying, "Honey, I'm back, ready to buy?" Most sales took 3-6 months just to get started.

V: What happened in the end?

SS: A few more years went by as the company struggled to recoup its investment. It never did. The division was sold off, and the company took a financial hit which served as a tax write-off. Many senior executives lost their jobs. The only satisfying moment was when the CFO was terminated. But it was too little, too late. It was a different kind of green that brought this division down: envy. So when I tell you there are people in the company who will undermine your success, I'm not being fatalistic, I'm being realistic.

V: You've made your point. Did you make a lot of money in commissions?

SS: Damn right. When you sell, you expect to get paid and paid well.

V: How much did you make in your best year?

SS: That's a little personal, don't you think? What difference does it make how much I made? Any answer I give won't make anyone sell better.

V: Yeah, but it may give incentive to people in sales to work harder, or for those not in sales to get into sales.

SS: Here's all you need to know: When I was selling, I made damn good money. I didn't have to worry about what I bought; I only knew that I could. When I went into a store, I didn't have to ask 'how much.' My houses - yes, more than one - were paid for in cash. My cars, all cash. I lived a zero-debt life. Do you know what that is?

V: When you have no debts at all.

SS: You got it. And all people need to know is that sales is one of the few professions where you can control your own financial destiny. How much you make depends on how much you hustle and out-hustle others to get the business.

V: Did you ever worry about not having a job? Not being able to be in sales?

SS: Okay, YOU are legally insane. It should be you strapped in this jacket, shackled to the wall. Listen closely. A great salesperson *never* has to worry about job security. If you're that good, someone will always hire you. This great economic engine cannot exist without the salesperson. I once heard an anecdote about a man who was about to go bankrupt. He said, "Take my lawyers, accountants, secretary, workers and others, but leave me my salespeople. With them I will rebuild."

V: It was just a question.

SS: (Rolling his eyes and shaking his head in disapproval)

V: Let's go back to compensation for a bit and talk about sales quotas. What motivates you? Is it the commission, the thrill of the sale, awards, what?

SS: It's not the money. Well, maybe at first it is. But after a while, it's much more than that.

V: What do you mean?

SS: If I were to describe the ideal sales gig, it would go something like this: selling great products, working for a great company and making great money. That's the trifecta. That's the winning triangle. If all three of those are in balance, the sales experience as a whole is enjoyable

V: I'd agree with you on that.

SS: I wasn't asking for your approval.

V: Asshole.

SS: Good for you. You can swear. You're human after all.

V: So I was asking what motivates you.

SS: Oh yeah. Well, having a great product to sell makes the sales experience more pleasant. Knowing you have a great product allows you to sell with confidence, and in the game of sales, it's all about maintaining a high level of confidence.

V: What about salespeople who sell not so great products? You mentioned they can still be successful.

SS: Yes, I did say that because it does happen. What I didn't say is whether or not they were happy selling their inferior wares. A salesperson has to believe in the product. Has to buy into it if he's going to sell it.

V: So you would agree with the adage that a salesman has to be sold on the product himself before he can succeed in selling it?

SS: I would agree with the statement and add to it. A salesperson who believes in his or her product is a more dangerous competitor than a salesperson with a better product but who lacks belief in the product. Customers look to see if you believe what you're telling and selling.

V: So your mindset is, if they don't like their own product – don't believe in it – they won't be good at selling.

SS: Right on the money. I once heard a story about the best harmonica salesman in the world. Nobody could outsell this guy, and every year he picked up his award at the annual sales meeting. One day, on a routine sales call, he was asked by a potential client if the harmonica, which played in a particular key, was available in other keys as well. The salesman was taken aback, because no one had ever asked him that question. He called the home office to check on it, only to find out that their harmonicas were designed to play in one key and one key only. From that point on, the salesman no longer believed his product to be the best on the market. And no sooner than he lost his faith in the product, his confidence and along with it his ability to sell were undermined. After that fateful day, he was no longer the number one salesperson in the company. Now replace the harmonica in this example with what you're selling.

V: Do salespeople underestimate the customer's perception?

SS: Many do at their own peril. You can only fake it up to a point. If you know and believe in your product, your client will sense it – maybe not intellectually, but they will feel it in their guts that you're bullshitting them. And once their BS alarm goes off, trying to sell becomes an uphill battle.

V: Much like Sisyphus?

SS: God bless you.

V: No, I mean the titan who was punished for his trickery by the gods. Sisyphus was compelled to roll a huge rock up a steep hill, but every time he'd get close to the top of the hill, the rock always escaped him and he had to begin again.

SS: I guess you can look at it that way.

V: So having a great product is a plus. What about your organization?

SS: You have to have a good support structure in place to succeed in sales. It starts with top management all the way down to the front line customer support person. You can sell like mad, no pun intended, but if you don't have a structure to sell, ship and support your products, you'll have problems in the long run.

V: What makes a good top sales management team, from your experience?

SS: Salespeople need guidance the most. A good sales management team can provide the type of guidance that will shortcut or fast track a salesperson's success. Salespeople, if I may be blunt, are fair-weather friends. When they're making money, they're happy. When they're not, management is to blame.

V: Really?

SS: Yes, sir. That's the way it is. Salespeople care about only one thing at the end of the year: how much money did they make. They care about what they helped make for the company to the extent they got paid for it.

V: Sounds egotistical.

SS: You have to be somewhat egotistical to be in sales. I've never met an ego-less salesperson. The confidence to overcome objections and rejection requires a character that can withstand criticism and be apathetic to praise.

V: That's a strange notion, 'apathetic to praise.'

SS: Think about it. Salespeople care about how much they're selling, which will tell them how much they'll make. You can praise them all you want for their tenacity, persistence and sales skills, but it won't make a difference to a seasoned veteran. When you first start out, people will tell you how great you are and how much they value you. But over time, you realize you can't deposit praise or accolades in the bank to pay off your bills.

V: That's an interesting perspective.

SS: You know, I hate when people respond with 'interesting.' When I hear 'interesting,' I take that to mean either you're really thinking about what I just said, or you didn't give a rip and ignored what I just said. Which is it? Nine times out of ten, it's the latter.

V: No, really, it's interesting in the thoughtful sense, using accolades and praise as metaphors for money. I've never heard anyone put it quite like that, so I had to give it some thought.

SS: I believe you.

V: So it's more about money than praise.

SS: I'll agree to that, but I need to make sure it's framed within the right context. If a salesperson makes a lot of money and gets praise on top of it, that's just icing on the cake of a great year financially. If a salesperson gets praise but doesn't make any money, that's just kicking sand in his eyes.

V: Why is praising him like kicking sand in his eyes? I don't get it.

SS: The contradiction is staring you right in the face, Sigmund. If you praise salespeople and tell them how great they are and how much the company values their service, they may feel good for a while. But the reality of not being able to afford things creates this conflicted dualism.

V: Stop calling me Sigmund. And since when did a salesperson ever take the time to understand the concept of dualism?

SS: Okay, try this. On the one hand, you tell him he's good and on the other hand you don't compensate him for being good. What is he supposed to think?

V: I don't know.

SS: Exactly. That's why praise without some type of reward to me is worthless when it comes to long-term results. You can tell a bum he's the greatest soul in the world, but his reality while sleeping on a steel grate to stay warm at night stands in stark contrast to what you're telling him.

V: So you're saying praise doesn't work?

SS: No, I'm saying praise is a placebo. It's only effective as long as the patient believes it's helping him. But when he realizes it's not, the placebo is no longer effective. Praise and accolades become ineffective the moment the salesperson realizes he's not making any real money being a great guy!

V: So you will always choose the money?

SS: Every fucking time! I can't put it any plainer than that!

V: Would you say a good manager is one that takes care of his or her salesmen?

SS: No, the great manager is one that positions the good salesperson to make good money. There is no ensuring or guarantees in this business. As a manager, your goal is to help the salesperson make as much money as he or she can because that translates into the company and the manager making a lot of money. It's a win-win-win: salesperson, management and company.

V: I agree. Tell me about some of your compensation plans that you've really liked and benefited from.

SS: One Fortune 500 company I worked for had it right. They understood the true nature of the salesperson, how he functions, and they tailored the compensation plan to drive their sales force. Every year the compensation program got better. Sometimes it was half a percentage point here or some bonus milestone there. They were exceptionally creative when it came to keeping the sales force focused on making more sales. They were able to create what I call a 'sales force frenzy.'

V: What's that mean?

SS: By having fresh incentives, everyone on the sales force got more motivated to sell. So much so that it became a competition to outsell the other salespeople. The competition was mostly friendly, because in the end we all wanted to see the company hit its annual target revenue. When the company hit its target, we'd all win somehow. So although we were competitors trying to outsell the other, we knew that what ultimately mattered was the sum total of all our efforts.

V: Sounds ideal.

SS: Don't know if I'd call it ideal, but it was pretty damn close. Every year new twists were added to perpetuate the camaraderie and, at the same time, instigate a competitive environment. The company added many spiffs –

V: What's a spiff?

SS: A spiff is something thrown in in addition to the commissions made on sales. A spiff directs your sales efforts. For example, if a new product was released, the first person to sell X dollars worth would get a cash prize. Or the first person to penetrate a major account with this new product was awarded another cash prize. Spiffs are creative, motivational sales tools that allow managers to direct our sales efforts.

V: Sounds like they kept it highly competitive. You would think in that type of environment that people would be tempted to cheat the system somehow to get more commissions. Did that ever happen?

SS: Each salesperson had his own territory, so there were few occasions when anyone was ever accused of double dipping.

V: Double dipping?

SS: You sell in your territory; that's one dip. And then you go over to another person's territory without them knowing and steal some business; that's the second dip.

V: Did double dipping ever happen?

SS: Oh yeah. This is where a good strong manager comes in. First, the rules of engagement were clear: double dipping is not allowed. Second, if double dipping was discovered, the guilty salesperson would lose the sales and forfeit any commission drawn from those sales. Our managers were tough. If you were caught double dipping, it was like the scarlet letter. Everyone on the team would avoid you and not speak to you. This type of culture encourages people to play it straight.

V: Did salespeople ever get downsized?

SS: Downsized? I hate that politically correct term. I think you meant to ask me if people caught double dipping got fired. Fired! Is that what you meant?

V: Yes.

SS: Then yes, people got fired. First came being ostracized for double dipping and then eventually came the firing.

V: How did the salespeople feel about this Machiavellian style of management?

SS: We loved it. Those who played by the rules and were great salesmen didn't need to cheat or double dip. When management fired a DD – a double dipper – it sent a clear message that management was on guard and, more importantly, they were there to make sure everyone got their fair share of the sales pie. Knowing this allowed us to sell without fear or paranoia, thinking about whether or not someone from our side was stealing our business.

V: It had to be tough on management to make these termination decisions.

SS: I don't think so. I think if the evidence was there, the decision to fire someone was swift and with conviction. I believe it was Walt Disney who said, "Decisions are easy when morals are clear." You can't say it any better than that. Managers gave out the rules. Violators were reprimanded, then terminated if they didn't learn their lesson. We loved it!

V: I see.

SS: And I disagree with your mischaracterization of this management style as Machiavellian. If you define Machiavellian as swift and decisive, then I'm inclined to agree with you. But a real Machiavellian decision is a harsh action taken without care or consideration for anyone else involved. This is the opposite of what we're discussing here. The managers had the best interests of those who served them in mind: the salespeople.

V: Did you ever have any Machiavellian managers who had their own best interests in mind and not the salespersons'?

SS: Earlier on, I mentioned the time accounting got into the sales side and limited the amount of money salespeople could make, leading to poor sales and eventually the downfall of the product line. A good sales manager would've never let it get that far, let alone happen, in the first place. Good sales managers are always looking out for their team and putting them in a position to make money. Notice I didn't say *giving* them money; they still have to go out and earn it.

V: What if you don't have the best product?

SS: Again, you make do with what you're selling or find another company to work for, because if you don't believe in what you're selling, your numbers and poor performance will reflect that over time.

V: So a good manager's job is to help the salesmen make money doing what they do best, selling?

SS: I know it sounds complicated, Einstein, but that's it.

V: Have you ever been in a situation where a manager hasn't taken care of you?

SS: "How do I love thee, let me count the ways." I don't know who said that, but my sales version goes like this: "Let me screw thee, how do I count the ways."

V: I take it, it's happened often?

SS: I'll give you an example. While selling for a company one day, I was informed via the grapevine that my territory was to be switched. In other words, the territory I was cultivating was to be reassigned to another. I didn't believe the rumors until the vice president of sales called me into his office to lower the boom. I protested and asked why. He couldn't give me a good answer and reassured me that the new territory would be just as good, if not better. To which I responded, "If that's the case, give it to the other guy and let him work it." He refused. His mind was made up. He couldn't go back, especially after he informed the other salesperson that he would get the territory. Within two weeks, I quit.

V: You quit? Because of that?

SS: It wasn't just that. You make it sound like it was not a big thing.

V: It sounds like it's something to get mad about, but not quit.

SS: Do you believe good character in a person is important?

V: Yes.

SS: Do you believe that a relationship without mutual respect is doomed?

V: I would have to say yes again.

SS: It wasn't so much that he switched my territory, but how he did it. One, he made a decision without consulting me first. Two, after spending the last year cultivating the territory, I was looking forward to a great year. With the new territory, I would have to start all over again. This was the equivalent of taking money out of my pocket. Three, he told the other salesman it was a done deal before even speaking to me. That was the straw that broke this camel's back. If you have respect for another person, you would never make a decision that would impact that person without discussing it with him first.

V: I see your point.

SS: To me, this incident revealed his character. Many told me to watch my back, but I refused to believe the rumors about how he managed. He had never given me reason to question his leadership. But this incident showed me that he would do anything to make a buck no matter who got hurt. And if he did it once, he'd do it again without hesitation.

V: It's like that saying, "Screw me once, shame on you. Screw me twice, shame on me." For allowing it to happen again.

SS: Exactly. This was not the first time he'd done that to someone on the sales force. This time it was my turn, and I took it as a sign of professional disrespect.

V: Did you ever regret quitting?

SS: Fuck no! I told you, a great salesperson never has to worry about getting a job. Within three weeks, I was working for a competitor.

V: What was the company's reaction?

SS: When I tendered my resignation, many in upper management tried to convince me to stay. They all knew I was given a raw deal. But my mind was made up; I was gone. Once you lose trust in your sales manager, it's only a matter of time before something gives.

V: What happened when they found out you went to work for a competitor?

SS: Oh, they weren't happy campers. 'Pissed off' would be an appropriate description. I heard through the grapevine – old friends – that the vice president planned on suing my new company if they didn't fire me, but nothing ever came of it.

V: How did you do against your old company?

SS: About a year later, after I'd wreaked much havoc on my old company's sales numbers, they decided to strike a deal with the company I was with and join forces to sell our products.

V: Let me see if I understand. Your old company began losing sales, so they set up a contract with your new company to help stave off the falling sales.

SS: Yeah, there's more to it than that, but that's the general idea. You know what they say, "If you can't beat 'em, join 'em."

V: That must've been very satisfying for you.

SS: Damn right! Revenge can be a real bitch, which is why you should always watch who you screw. Like a boomerang, it can come back and smack you in the head when you least expect it.

V: Did you ever run into your old manager, the vice president, again?

SS: A few times. He refused to speak to me and, in some cases, acknowledge my presence.

V: What did you do?

SS: The same thing! I didn't care if he spoke to me or not. He was no longer part of my sales reality, therefore, not relevant. In the sales game, you have to remain to some degree emotionless. You can't wear your heart on your sleeve or people will rip it off every time. I would've taken his snub personally, but since I didn't care, it didn't matter how he reacted.

V: I guess so. If you could talk to him today, what would be your advice based on what happened?

SS: Managers need to understand that there are certain things you don't do to salespeople who are producing for you. You can't change their territory if it will impact their sales number, their commission, and you can't change their incentive plans (like reducing their commission rate), especially when the company is doing well. Any way you cut it, both of these maneuvers are equivalent to putting your hand into the salesman's pocket and taking his money. Nothing will set a salesperson against a company faster than messing with his or her cash flow.

Transcript Note > Attempting to evaluate the inmate's level of loyalty towards a company.

V: That fact that you can walk away from a company with which you are in disagreement brings up another subject: loyalty.

SS: Yeah, what about it?

V: Do you believe in corporate loyalty?

SS: No.

V: No?

SS: You heard me. What were you expecting, some lengthy diatribe about the virtues of loyalty?

V: I don't know what I was expecting, but a quick 'no' wasn't it. Tell me why you don't believe in corporate loyalty. Are you telling me you're simply devoid of loyalty when it comes to business?

SS: Loyalty in business is a bunch of bullshit. Every time I see books written about loyalty or people praising the virtue of loyalty, I want to fucking puke. I heard a speaker talk about loyalty for about an hour once; I never heard such horseshit in my life.

V: Help me understand your rejection of loyalty in business.

SS: Well, what is loyalty?

V: Being faithful to some company or person no matter how tough things get.

SS: I never understood the notion of loyalty in business. To me, business loyalty is an oxymoron, emphasis on the 'moron.'

V: Why so? Most people think that loyalty in business is a good thing.

SS: Most people are fucked up if they think that. Years of conditioning have people accepting without question the very premise of the concept of loyalty.

V: Explain.

SS: As children we are told that loyalty is very important. You should be loyal to your friends. You should be loyal to your family members. You should be loyal to your teammates, and so on. Ironically enough, dogs are held up as the most loyal creatures. If that isn't fucked up, I don't know what is.

V: I don't understand.

SS: I call it the 'Lassie Effect.' You can kick a dog. Beat a dog. Starve a dog. Even shoot the dog in the leg, but in the end, that dog is still loyal. So when someone says we should be loyal, are they seriously asking us to put up with what the dog has put up with and still love our 'torturer?' Get real! If a boss treats you like shit, pays you shit and makes you eat shit every time you suggest something, are you telling me I as an employee should be loyal?

V: No, not under those circumstances. But I think you're pointing out an extreme case.

SS: Listen to yourself. Are you implying that there are grades of loyalty? If he kicks you, beats you, shoots you, you shouldn't be loyal. But if he only kicks you, well now, let's still be loyal. Is that what you're saying? You're shitting me, right?

V: Now you're putting words in my mouth.

SS: Welcome to my world!

V: Let's step back for a second. Let's not talk about dogs; we're talking about human beings. I'm talking about working for a company that has not only trained and educated you, but has provided you with a good means to support yourself. Are you telling me you would have no loyalty toward this company after it treated you this well?

SS: Do me a favor, take that pen and shove it up your ass, because it's going to be less painful than what I'm about to tell you. That is, if you can handle some reality?

V: I'm listening.

SS: When you describe this ideal job, with an ideal boss who's paying me an ideal wage, I can't tell if you have a great sense of imagination or great sense of humor.

V: Okay, all jobs are not ideal. Get to the point. I want your take on loyalty.

SS: Here's my take on loyalty. Loyalty is for suckers. Before you jump down my throat, let me ask you a few questions, then I'll make my point.

V: Go.

SS: When a company begins to lose money because a product isn't selling, does a company shoulder the loss and not fire anyone, or does it 'downsize' to adjust to market realities?

V: I assume it has to downsize.

SS: When a company is not making money and shareholders are yelling at the CEO, does the CEO in the majority of cases listen to his shareholders, or does he shoulder the financial burden?

V: Given that most CEOs don't own the company, they're probably going to buckle under to the demands of their shareholders.

SS: So would you agree with the statement that if the market is not being too kind to a company, and sales are down, the company will let some of its employees go to reduce costs?

V: I can't argue with that; they'll rightsize the company.

SS: Rightsize, that's code for firing people until we stop losing money. Am I right?

V: I guess.

SS: Fuck you, you know I'm right. There's no guessing here. Companies will downsize a company to reduce costs in a down market. No ifs, ands or buts. So my question to you is: Where is the corporate loyalty?

V: Well ...

SS 'Well' my ass, you know damn well there's no such thing as corporate loyalty when a company begins to lose money. All lofty ideals of corporate paternalism vanish when corporate profits diminish. You can't argue with that, you just can't!

V: I don't have an argument.

SS: Have you ever read a gentleman by the name of Jean Jacques Rousseau? He wrote a book called *The Social Contract*?

V: No.

SS: You need to hit the bookstore more often. Rousseau talked about the nature of man and how we enter into social contracts with each other in order to maintain social order. I view employment with another company as a social contract. You said earlier that I should be appreciative of a company who provides me employment, a good environment and a decent wage. You have your head up your ass on this one. I'd turn it around and answer you that a company should be appreciative that I am lending my talent to make them productive and profitable. You see, when a company employs you, they aren't doing you a favor – they're doing what's in their best interest! And that is to hire people to help them make money. So if you ask me, do I feel indebted to a company who employs me, I would respond in kind by asking you if they shouldn't feel indebted that I am lending them my services for a fee.

V: So you see yourself as a commodity, a product to be bought on the open market for a price?

SS: Ah! You're starting to understand me. I see myself not only as a commodity, but much more than that. A commodity is a product that is readily available, and because it's available in volumes it's also inexpensive. You see, I view my sales talent as not so readily available in the market. You just can't find good salespeople anywhere. Great salespeople are hard to find. And because they're hard to find, they're more valuable.

V: So you see yourself as a high-end product?

SS: You're getting there. I see myself as a person who brings to the table a set of valuable skills not readily available in the market. So if a company wants to hire me, I don't see them as being superior or in the driver's seat; quite the contrary. I see them as equal to what I'm offering. In other words, I'm not thinking, "I wonder if they'll hire me?" No. I'm thinking, "Will this company help me make a lot of money selling?"

V: That seems a little cold and materialistic.

SS: No! I see myself as a specialist, an expert with certain skills companies want. And if they want it, they'll have to convince me it's in my best interest to work for them. The only reason you're having a problem grasping what I'm telling is because you've been conditioned to 'look' for a job. I've learned to look for opportunities.

V: I'm not sure I understand your point.

SS: Did you ever see any Clint Eastwood westerns?

V: Of course.

SS: In some of these westerns, Clint is the fastest gun alive and people want to hire him for his talent. Clint has to weigh whose offer he'll accept. He's not thinking about loyalty. He's not thinking about what the organization is selling. His only concern is what will put him in the best position to make the most money. He's all about maximizing profit and opportunity. He's a hired gun.

V: So you see yourself as a hired gun as a salesperson?

SS: Bingo! I am a hired gun. My contract with any company, if it could be written, would go along these lines: I will sell a company's product in exchange for commissions. I give them 40 hours a week, so to speak, and they give me what I've earned. At the end of the week or month, we settle up. My obligation to any company ends there.

V: It's hard to argue with your logic.

SS: I love your choice of word, 'logic.' If I believed in loyalty, it would be rational loyalty. I will remain loyal to a company as long as it makes sense for both parties, them and me. Once it stops making sense for either side, dissolution of the agreement should occur.

V: So every relationship in your opinion should be based on a mutually beneficial state?

SS: Yes.

V: What about customer loyalty? People who've bought from you in the past? Should they remain loyal to you?

SS: No.

V: What? Are you telling you don't expect customers to be loyal?

SS: Absolutely not. That would be contradictory to what I just explained. Every relationship has to be mutually beneficial, a win-win. As soon as someone's not benefiting, that person or entity has the right to terminate the relationship.

V: I'm not buying it. You're telling me you don't care if a customer remains loyal to you or not?

SS: Caring is a feeling, an emotion. One of the things we salespeople can't afford to do is to tie ourselves emotionally to a client. Clients are renowned for stabbing you in the back as soon as some better product or pricing becomes available.

V: So customers themselves are not loyal?

SS: Customers are loyal as long as it is beneficial and convenient for them to be so. I can't count the number of times I serviced a client to the nines only to have them drop my product line for another because they offered better prices or more value.

V: Does that upset you?

SS: That a customer drops me for a better product? It bothers me, but it's understandable. A client's job is to look out for the best interest of his or her company, not to make me richer. If I'm selling a non-competitive, more expensive product, I can't expect a client to remain loyal to me when he or she has the fiduciary duty to look out for the company's best interest. So, no, it doesn't bother me. It just tells me that we, the company, are being out-marketed or out-priced by our competitors.

V: Alright. Good enough. I have a good sense of where you're coming from. So once you managed to get a good territory, how did you approach the business? What were some of your sales strategies for success? Let's assume you have a good product, a good compensation plan in hand and a decent territory.

SS: If I have these three things in place, I know that success is just a matter of executing a targeted strategy.

V: So before you started going out and meeting customers, you knew exactly who your buyers were?

SS: I had their profile down. The rest was a matter of stalking my prey and going in for the kill.

V: Where do you get their profile? Your hit list of clients to go after?

SS: There are several ways to develop a 'hit list,' as you call it. If I'm starting out with a new company or territory, I go straight to the history file. I find out what customers have bought in the last year or so. I then look at the products they've bought to give me an indication of what's selling and what's not. If I notice a particular product is selling, I ask myself why.

V: Before you jump to picking the product to push, stay on the subject of finding your clients.

SS: Pushy bastard. By looking at who bought in the last year, I try to compile the

following about the customer: Who are they?
How big are they? How often have they
bought? What market do they serve? From
here, I start categorizing them.

V: How do you do that?

SS: Well, I use the famous Pareto Principle
of Sales. Eighty percent of your business
will come from twenty percent of your
customers. So I use this 80/20 rule and
find my 20% who are buying. By studying
these top buyers, I'll begin to formulate a
profile of the type of company they are and
what types of products they're more likely
to buy, and most importantly, I try to
understand why they bought them.

V: So you think understanding the 'why'
behind the buy is important?

SS: This is what separates the catalog
openers from real salespeople. Catalog
openers just want to sell and don't give a
rip one way or another how the customer is
using the product. A real salesperson will
ask what the product will be used for and
why they decided to buy this particular
product. Understanding the use and function
the customer has in mind gives you great
insight into their business.

V: Why is that important?

SS: Think about it. If you understand what
the company is doing and why they're doing
it, you now have an insight into their
business plan. Understanding their thinking
will allow to do one of two things: First,
inform your marketing department of how the
products are being used and their long-term
intent, so they can begin incorporating any
necessary changes to their marketing
message. Second, if you're selling multiple

products, by understanding their business better you may be able to upsell them on other products your company has. Associative selling is one of the most powerful strategies in selling to existing customers.

V: Associative selling?

SS: You know, upselling. If you sold them one thing maybe you can sell them something else. The objective is to sell as much to a single customer as you can.

V: Sounds like a good strategy.

SS: You gotta be shitting me. It's fucking great strategy. When you walk into a fast food restaurant and ask for a hamburger, the cashier will ask you if you want fries with that. As soon as you say yes, they'll ask you if you want something to drink to wash that down. That's upselling. They're selling you as much as they can to maximize time, money and profit to the company. It's not just a good strategy, it's a killer strategy.

V: Got it, sell as much to one customer as you can.

SS: In business there's a figure thrown around that says it's six times cheaper to keep a customer than to go out and find a new one. Whether you agree or disagree with the number doesn't matter. What matters is that it will always be cheaper in terms of time, money and effort to sell to an existing customer than to find a new one.

V: Makes perfect sense.

SS: If it makes perfect sense, then why is it that many salespeople haven't figured this out? Instead, they're running around with their heads cut off trying to find new business when all the business they want is right at their feet. It reminds me of the story "Acres of Diamonds." Are you familiar with it?

V: No, I don't think so.

SS: It's a great story, told by the founder of Temple University, Russell Conwell. Let me share it with you.

There once lived a Persian by the name of Al Hafed who owned a very large farm. He was a contented and wealthy man -- contented because he was wealthy and wealthy because he was contented. One day an old priest came to visit, and as they sat down by the fire, the priest began to tell a story about a far away place with diamonds. The old priest told Al Hafed that if he had a handful of diamonds he could purchase a whole country, and with a mine of diamonds he could place his children upon thrones through the influence of their great wealth.
Al Hafed, upon hearing all about diamonds and how much they were worth, went to his bed that night a poor man -- not that he had lost anything, but poor because he was discontented and discontented because he thought he was poor. He said, "I want a mine of diamonds!" So he lay awake all night, and early in the morning sought out the priest.
He awoke the priest from his dreams and asked him, "Will you tell me where I can find diamonds?" The priest said, "Diamonds? What do you want with diamonds?" "I want to be immensely rich," said Al Hafed, "but I don't know where to go." "Well," said the priest, "if you find a river that runs over white sands between high mountains, in

those sands you will always see diamonds."
So he sold his farm, collected his money at
interest, left his family in the care of a
neighbor, and away he went in search of
diamonds.
He traveled the world trying to find those
diamonds. At last, when his money was all
spent, and he was in rags, wretched and
poor, he stood on the shore of a bay, cast
himself into the incoming tide and was
never seen again.

V: That's a depressing story. It makes no
sense.

SS: Wait, I'm not finished.

Al Hafed's successor at the farm led his
camel out into the garden to drink, and as
the camel put its nose down into the clear
water of the garden brook, the successor
noticed a curious flash of light from the
sands of the shallow stream. Reaching in,
he pulled out a black stone with an eye of
light that reflected all the colors of the
rainbow. He took that curious pebble into
the house and left it on the mantel, then
went on his way and forgot all about it.
A few days later, the old priest who told
Al Hafed where diamonds were found came in
to visit his successor. When he saw the
flash of light from the mantel, he rushed
up and said, "Here is a diamond! Has Al
Hafed returned?" "No, no, Al Hafed has not
returned and that is not a diamond; that is
nothing but a stone. We found it right out
here in our garden." "But I know a diamond
when I see it," said the priest. "That is a
diamond!"
Together they rushed to the garden and
stirred up the white sands with their
fingers and found others, more beautiful
and more valuable diamonds than the first,
and thus was discovered one of the most

*magnificent diamond mines in the history of
mankind.*

You see, sometimes the opportunity to make
money, be rich, is right there at our feet;
we just have to be wise enough to recognize
it.

V: You also have to know the difference
between a piece of charcoal and a diamond.

SS: That's called education. One of the
things I never stopped doing was learning.
No matter how many years in the business, I
always took time to attend seminars or read
a book. As I said before, those who want to
stay ahead of the sales game must
discipline themselves to stay current with
what's happening in the market.

V: On that note, when you're going after a
customer, how do you know if you have an
acre of diamonds or an acre of rocks? How
do you find the best opportunities to go
after, the 'diamonds' in your territory?

SS: You ever watched those crime dramas on
television where they have to figure out
what happened at the murder scene?

V: Yes, I have.

SS: What they do is piece together bits of
evidence to figure out the motive for the
crime. They also use the evidence to get a
profile of the likely suspect.

V: I see where you're going.

SS: Every crime has a motive. Every sale
has profit motive. Every sale should be
treated like a crime scene. Bring in
forensics to find the evidence of what
caused the sale. The best to place to start

looking for evidence is in the sales history. Look at what clients are buying, how much and when.

V: Walk me through your thought process if you were just starting out in a new territory.

SS: You start by getting the sales data for the last two years.

V: What should you collect?

SS: First, get a list of the top clients or customers who bought. I sort these first by year. So I list out who bought what and how much two years ago. Then I do the same thing for the past year. If the clients are consistent buyers, they should be in the top 20%. This immediately tells me that I have consistent buyers that I have to continue to nurture and where I can, upsell. I also look at how often they're buying during the year to give me an idea of their buying patterns from quarter to quarter.

V: So then you would begin by working the list of clients who have been buying?

SS: Absolutely. Remember, it's easier to sell to an existing client than to go out and find a new one. So what I would do is figure out what they've already bought and then work up a list of other products I may be able to sell them.

V: What if they're not in the top 20% from two years ago to the past year?

SS: Something's wrong. If the sales are dropping, I want to know why. Is the customer company losing market share? If so, can our products help them regain some market share? Did their sales process or purchasing folks change? Did they start buying from our competitors? Do they not like our products? Is our service bad? There are a lot of questions that have to be asked to ascertain why the sales have declined from one year to the next. This is where you have to go into investigative mode and figure out how the crime was committed.

V: What crime?

SS: Look, when you start losing sales from one year to another, that's criminal. You should never let that happen if you can prevent it. You need to find out immediately what's happening.

V: And you think the best way to do that is study the history?

SS: Again, think like an investigator. You've found evidence that a crime (no sales) was committed. You now have to go interview the suspects to get the real picture of what's happening.

V: Where do you start?

SS: By rounding up the usual suspects and asking the person who has either managed or worked the territory in the past. If they're not available, I go to management and try to get answers. By this time I have an idea of what was happening from the company's perspective.

V: Why not go see the clients directly?

SS: Slow your roll, big boy, I'm getting there. Before you go poking your nose in a client's place of business, you need to know *your* business. Never go see a client for the first time without understanding the history of the client. I've seen many a rookie go ask the client, "What's the matter? You're not buying from us." Mistake. Big Mistake! The client's job is not to educate you. It's your job as a salesperson to understand them. Second, never walk in asking questions you don't know the answers to. That's an accident waiting to happen.

V: What do you mean?

SS: If you go in there asking, "Why have you stopped buying?," you may hear something like, "Well, your company never reason 1, reason 2 or reason 3. When we had problems, you never problem 1, problem 2 or problem 3. And that's why we don't buy from you." Now what are you going to do? How do you answer these questions if you didn't take the time to research it? What are you going to say – "Uh, I'll have to get back to you?"

V: What's wrong with getting back to them?

SS: Don't think like a dipshit. You've set up a meeting with a past client who's not buying. This means they have to stop what they're doing to meet with you. You then go meet with them and the best answer you have to their question is, "I'll get back to you?" They're going to think you're a moron, and your company must be moronic for hiring you. Not only have you wasted your time, you've wasted the client's time. Setting up the next meeting will be difficult because one, their time is valuable and you just wasted it. Two, why would they want to do business with a company that hasn't taken the time or made the effort to understand the history of the relationship?

V: Maybe if you're a smooth talker –

SS: Shut up! I'm tired of slick salespeople who think they can talk themselves out of anything. They assume the customer is gullible enough to buy their bullshit. Don't underestimate your customer's sense of perception or their level of tolerance. Smart salespeople never bullshit. You try to dance your way through a meeting without preparing, you're asking to get your ass handed to you.

V: Slick doesn't sell?

SS: Slick is a short-term strategy. Yeah, you may be able to pull the wool over the customer's eyes once in a while. But is that the reputation a salesperson wants to develop? Eventually the bullshit catches up with you, and you've just undermined your sales career. Nothing can replace the sincere effort of caring for what your customer needs and then going about your business to help them fill that need. Fancy dinners and a day at the golf course will only get you so far.

V: So if you do your homework first, then what? How do you go about setting up a meeting, and with whom? Tell me about your approach.

SS: One of the things all great salespeople try to figure out is who is writing the checks – who are the decision makers. I try to find old meeting notes to see who attended the last presentations, by going through files for memos or e-mails.

V: What if there is no paper trail, no files?

SS: I try to find past orders or invoices and see who the contact person in Purchasing was and start there. If that doesn't exist, you go back to the basics and make a phone call.

V: Who do you call?

SS: Think about it, you idiot. If you know your product, you should have a good idea of who the typical buyer in a company would be. Just use some common sense.

V: Okay, assume I'm an idiot and I don't have common sense; help me out here.

SS: Let God help you, I can't. I'm a salesman, not a miracle worker.

V: Okay, that didn't help. Who do you call if you don't know where to start?

Transcript Note > Interviewee discusses calling a company to find key decision makers.

SS: Start at the top and work your way down.

V: You mean call the president of the company?

SS: Yep, gotta start somewhere.

V: C'mon. You wouldn't call the president, really? Why not start lower?

SS: Huge mistake! If you're going to find a decision maker for your product or service, always work from the top down if you're going in blind. If you start at the bottom and work your way up, you just encounter non-decision makers who'll hand you off just to get rid of you. Or they'll keep promising you that they'll meet with you or call you back, but they never do. One way to ensure you not only get the right person but a meeting as well is to call the chief. If you get to talk to the president and he recommends you speak with Mr. X, I can assure you Mr. X will take your call and be willing to set up a meeting. Plus, you walk in with more cachet knowing that the president is aware of the meeting, which means his subordinates will listen to you and treat you better.

V: I still don't see why you can't work your way up.

SS: Let me tell you about a sales friend who tried calling at the bottom and working his way up. A salesman by the name of Raul was in the business of helping companies save money on their taxes. His expertise was finding tax write-offs most accountants and tax lawyers couldn't find. Raul was a non-salaried salesman who only made money when he saved the client company money.

V: How'd that work?

SS: If he could save the company, say, $200,000 a year in taxes, Raul would collect a ten percent bonus of $20,000.

V: Wow, sounds like great gig.

SS: Yeah, but you have to work hard to earn that commission. So Raul would call on companies to see if he could find the right person. His logic concluded that he should start with the accountants or tax lawyers. For two or three months, they'd give him the runaround by setting up meetings and then canceling them or not returning his calls.

V: What did he do?

SS: He didn't know what to do. He called me up and invited me to breakfast. It was then that he told me what he was trying to do and what was happening. He was frustrated and asked for my advice. I told him, he was never going to get these people to let him help them.

V: Why not? It's in their best interest.

SS: Don't be such a sucker.

V: What?

SS: Think about it. Those accountants or tax lawyers would never let a guy like him come in and help them save money. Because if Raul did show them how to save money, that would mean they're not doing their jobs. And there is no way those guys are going to let Raul show them he knows more about legal tax evasion then they do.

V: But if he's saving the company money, don't they have fiduciary responsibility to act in the best interest of the company?

SS: On principle you're right, but that doesn't mean most people are principle-oriented. If these guys let Raul come in and show them up, they could jeopardize their jobs. So principle in this case is trumped by the most basic survival instinct man has, self-preservation. They're more interested in saving their jobs than moving the company forward.

V: Did you encounter this in sales as well?

SS: You bet! Many people have a vested interest in maintaining the status quo. Change scares them. Salespeople are agents of change when we go into a company talking about a new product or service. The fear of change is a catalyst for people to act in their own interest and ignore what's in the best interest of a company.

V: So what did you do when you were blocked?

SS: I did what I told Raul to do: start calling at the top and work your way down. Within two weeks he had a meeting with the president of the company, who was excited when he realized how much money he could save the company per year. The president then contacted the company's tax lawyer, who was now accommodating and more than happy to cooperate with Raul to get the tax savings in place.

V: Was he able to save the company a lot of money?

SS: I don't recall the number, but Raul said he saved the company the equivalent of what you would pay five employees. So his tax reduction saved five jobs within the company. Something that wouldn't have happened if he kept trying to work with the accountant and the tax lawyer.

V: That's what's wrong with people when they let self-interest get in the way.

SS: No, self-interest is a good thing. In fact, all salespeople, all great salespeople, live the creed of self-interest.

V: Now you've confused me. You just told me how self-interest almost cost a company a lot of money.

SS: I told you no such thing. You called it self-interest, not me. I think what you meant to say is that the accountant and tax lawyer were selfish.

V: What's the difference, they're both the same thing.

SS: There's a big difference. Being selfish is when someone acts in their own best interest regardless of how it impacts others.

V: And self-interest isn't the same?

SS: We are all motivated into action by self-interest. Everything we do is because of self-interest. But when you act in your own best interest, you do so with the intent of not harming or impacting others. In fact, you may in some cases not only benefit from the act, but help others as a result of helping yourself.

V: I don't know if I get it.

SS: You decide to go to the corner to buy yourself an ice cream cone. You're going because you are interested in satiating your desire for something cold and sweet. If you steal the ice cream cone, that's selfish because it will negatively impact another – in this case the ice cream man, who'll have to pay for it out of his pocket. If you purchase the ice cream cone, there is no negative impact to anyone else; in fact, the ice cream man makes a little money.

V: So Raul was acting out of self-interest, because not only did he benefit from the tax savings but so did the company?

SS: Yes. Take it one step further. If Raul's tax saving strategies were illegal, he would still make money, but he would jeopardize the stability of the company. That would be selfish.

V: I see. I'm with you. Let me move on to the next logical step, then. Now that you knew to call at the top and work your way down, how did you do it? How did you get through to the president? They usually have secretaries to screen the calls.

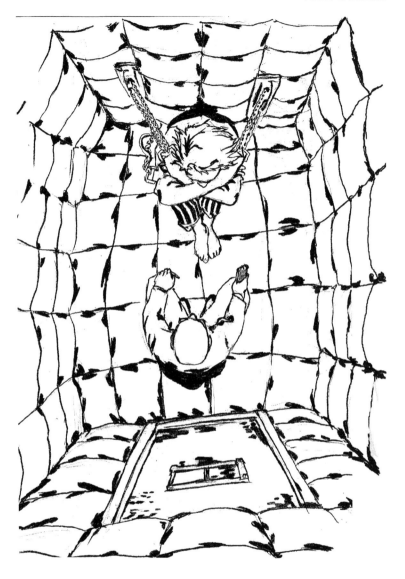

Transcript Note > Interviewee discusses cold calling and getting past the gatekeepers.

SS: How do you get past the secretaries, or what we call the 'gatekeepers?'

V: Yes.

SS: Well, a simple cold call with a little finesse can go a long way. The first thing you need to do is develop a list of people or leads you want to call on, and then see if you can set up a face to face meeting.

V: I've heard cold calling doesn't work.

SS: It's all a numbers game. The more you call, the more likely you are to gain business or, in this case, access to a top-level executive. The inverse holds true also. The aim of cold calling is to turn a long list of leads into a long list of meetings, into a long list of sales so you can get a long list of zeros behind your earnings. Simply stated, you need to convert your stack of leads into a stack of cash using your telephone. You're familiar with the Law of Probability?

V: Yes.

SS: Another way of viewing the cold calling process is to use the Law of Probability, which directly addresses your chances of success in a given activity. You can calculate the probability of success, the likelihood of the outcome you want, if you understand how your chances improve with every attempt.

V: You must be a gambler.

SS: No, idiot, not every salesperson you meet goes out drinking and gambling. In college we studied the laws of probability and how they were calculated. The example I remember best is the sack with the colored balls.

V: Never heard of it.

SS: In a sack there were ten balls. Nine of the ten were white and one was green. The professor started out by asking, What is the probability of you reaching into the bag and pulling out a green ball?

V: I don't know.

SS: The probability of you getting the green ball, which he described as P(g), was easily calculated by taking the number of green balls (one), dividing it by the total amount of balls in the sack (ten), and then multiplying it by one hundred.

V: Say that again.

SS: Here, write this down.

$P(g) = 1/10 = .10 \times 100 = 10\%$

V: Got it.

SS: Therefore, the chance of you pulling a green ball out of the sack on the first try is 10%. Not a bad probability, but not great.

V: I'm with you.

SS: So let's say you reach into the sack and pull out a white ball, leaving nine balls in the sack with the green one still in there. Now, what's the probability of you pulling out a green ball on the next try is calculated?

V: Uh, let me think.

SS: It's simple. Write this down.

P(g) = 1/9 = .11 x 100 = 11%

V: Alright.

SS: So your chances of getting a green ball improved slightly from 10% to 11%. It isn't a great improvement, but an improvement nonetheless. If you keep going, you'll begin to see what happens to your chances of getting the green ball as you continue to pull white balls out of the sack. Let's assume the green ball is pulled out last.

V: Why last?

SS: Because in sales, getting the right person may take ten tries. You could get lucky and get the green ball on the first try. As you keep pulling more white balls out of the sack, your chances of getting the green ball increase dramatically. To really understand it, calculate each probability until you finally pull out the green ball.

V: Give me a moment to write this out.

SS: Take your time, I'm not going anywhere.

(pause)

V: Here, take a look at this. How's that look?

SCRATCH PAD

White Balls	Green Balls	Total in Sack	Probability P(g)	P(g)x 100 %
9	1	10	.10	10%
8	1	9	.11	11%
7	1	8	.12	12%
6	1	7	.14	14%
5	1	6	.16	16%
4	1	5	.20	20%
3	1	4	.25	25%
2	1	3	.33	33%
1	1	2	.50	50%
0	1	1	1.0	100%

SS: Nice. You got it. As you can see from the table, your probability of getting a green ball out of the sack dramatically increases after the sixth ball is pulled, leaving only four in the sack. In the last row of the table, there are zero white balls left and only one green ball. So the chances of you pulling out a green ball with only one ball left are 100%. If you move up a row where there is one white ball and one green ball left in the sack, you can see that your chances of getting a green ball are 50%, a 50-50 chance.

V: Okay, thanks for the math lesson. But how does this apply to cold calling an executive or someone in a high position?

SS: You're welcome. It's all about prospecting.

V: Prospecting?

SS: Cold calling clients until you find one or more that is willing to meet with you. Prospecting is all about converting a stack of leads into a stack of cash. So let's drop the 't' in stack and think of a sack. In your sack, you have all these leads. Every time you pull a lead out of your sack and make a call, the probability of you getting an appointment or sale increases with every lead you pull. The green ball here symbolizes cash, money, orders. In sales you have to keep making those calls, and eventually the green ball is bound to turn up!

V: So how would you define prospecting?

SS: Prospecting is going out and finding new clients who'll buy your products or services.

V: I once read that most salespeople – or businesspeople for that matter – fail in the first year for lack of prospecting. Would you agree with that?

SS: Remember that movie with Kevin Costner, "Field of Dreams," where some spirit or force from baseball history is guiding him and telling him, "Build it and they will come?" We later find out that Costner's mission was to go out in the farmlands of Iowa and build a baseball field so two teams from the past can come back and play a game that was never played. Most salespeople in business have a "Field of Dreams" mindset when it comes to selling their products or services. They think now that they have a product or service to offer, customers will come knocking down their doors. Nothing could be further from the truth. You have to go out and get the business and not sit on your ass hoping someone will show up.

V: I would agree with you.

SS: Any marketer will tell you that you can have the greatest product or service in the world, but if no one knows about it, it might as well not exist in the first place. Success in business is about telling everyone you can about what you have to offer. You can spread the word through direct marketing, advertising, internet marketing, tradeshows, promotional events and so on. But one tool of marketing stands above the others as the most affordable, most accessible and the one that is hardly used: the telephone. The simple reason we hesitate to use the phone is that calling and asking for business makes us feel vulnerable.

V: Rejection is hard to take.

SS: Then get the hell out of sales if you can't handle rejection. Selling is the systematic elimination of rejections to get to one acceptance. I know that the simple act of asking in everyday life leaves us open and vulnerable to being rejected. But that's what sales is: asking.

V: Unless you're made of stone, rejection can undermine a person's confidence and self-esteem. Calling someone on the phone to ask for their business can be hard on a salesperson. You seem to be minimizing this effect on people.

SS: I'm not minimizing a damn thing. When we get rejected, we take it personally and that's where salespeople go wrong. The phone can be seen as an enabler to those feelings. You're right, by calling we are inviting rejection or opening ourselves to being told 'no' and consequently feeling bad. Given this association between 'calling' and feeling bad about oneself, it's no wonder we view the phone with disdain when it comes to making cold calls and soliciting business.

V: So how did you overcome your fear of cold calling?

SS: In cold calling, there are three entities involved: the client, the phone company and you, the caller. We know we can't control how a client will react to our call. We can't do anything about the telephone company since they are simply providing the means of communication. What we can control is how we view calling and how we handle a call and what we allow ourselves to think and feel. Therefore, the first rule of cold calling is never take anything personally. If a new client doesn't want to talk to you, they aren't rejecting you! I can prove it. When you call a client and they either don't take your call or refuse to talk to you, at that moment, they know nothing of you. So how could they reject you personally without knowing of you? They probably don't even know your name. It's not you they're rejecting, but your solicitation for their time or your proposition.

V: Yeah, that makes sense. You can't take it personally if they don't even know who you are. But how do you create that connection to get in the door?

SS: Herein lies the dilemma faced by salespeople. How can you present the value of your proposition and prove that it's worth their time if they won't give you the chance to explain it in the first place?

V: Exactly.

SS: Cold calling is the creative art of finding ways to create time with your potential client for you to explain the value of your proposition. It's no different than dating when you're trying to find a mate.

V: What?

SS: Don't get your panties in a bunch. Just let me digress for a second and draw a human parallel to illustrate my point. A man, interested in finding a mate, does the upfront, personalized version of cold calling. A man (i.e., a salesman) sees a woman (i.e., a prospect) he likes. He begins to think of a clever way to get her attention. He knows he has to have a great opening line, good conversation in the middle and a good close. The end goal is getting her to go out with him on a date (i.e., an appointment or meeting to further explain the benefits he offers with the hope that she buys into it). If the appointment (i.e., dinner) is set, the man has to ensure that the meeting place provides the right ambience conducive to productive conversation. Are you following this?

V: Yes, keep going.

SS: During their dinner, he will emphasize his features and explain or hint of their benefits. He may tell her about how he's a vice president in a Fortune 100 company. This would be considered a 'product' feature. The implied benefit is that if she buys into him, he can provide a financially stable situation. If he talks about how much he loves to go running (another feature), the implied benefit is that he's a healthy specimen and would be around for a while. As you can see, cold calling over the phone has its parallel with dating. Women are the clients and men are just salesmen trying to close a deal.

V: That's so crude!

SS: Not so fast. In this day and age, it wouldn't surprise me to see a man being 'prospected' by a woman. It cuts both ways today.

V: True.

SS: Let me push the analogy a little further. Cold calling is no different than trying to find a date, with the obvious exception that it's business and you have a product or service to sell. What makes cold calling different from trying to get a date is the medium. When a man sees a woman he's interested in, just by observing he is able to make a quick assessment of whether or not he wants to pursue the matter. He can look at her height, weight, hair color, eye color, her smile, how she dresses, how she walks, how she carries herself and so on. These are all visual cues you can't get over a phone.

V: Okay.

SS: What makes cold calling tough is that, over the phone, the information is sketchier. You don't know what the person looks like, so it's hard to assess who they are or might be. You can't see how they dress or how their office looks, which would give you some indication of their organizational skills or level in the company. When you ask a question, you can't see their reaction visually; you can only listen for the tone in their response. Would you agree with me so far?

V: Yes.

SS: Good. When you see someone, you can gather more information about the person. The person you're watching is, whether they're aware of it or not, broadcasting signals about who they are. Over the phone, the visual component is not available, so you are left with only their voice: their tone, vocabulary, the jargon they use, their sense of humor. This form of communication can be referred to as 'narrowcasting.'

V: You lost me.

SS: Narrowcasting, as opposed to broadcasting, provides less information because of the medium of communication, in this case the phone. I'll give you another example. People who use the Internet to chat with friends or strangers can also be said to be narrowcasting because you can't see the person's reaction to what you're saying; you have no visual cues. This is one of the reasons Internet users invented emoticons.

V: Emoticons?

SS: Emotional icons. You know, a colon and the right side of the parentheses make a sideways smile. The colon and the left side of the parentheses make a sideways frown. Peoples use them all the time on e-mail messages. Emoticons are a creative way to express emotions when you only have words to go on. It helps the other person understand the emotional state of the person writing the e-mail.

V: What does this have to do with cold calling?

SS: The lack of visual information while cold calling adds to our anxiety. We don't have the luxury of emoticons. When we can't see the person we're talking to, we feel uncomfortable because we don't know what they might be thinking. And, as the saying goes, in the absence of information we tend to make things up. We may start to think that the person on the other end of the phone really doesn't want to talk to us or would rather be doing something else. Since we can't tell, we begin to feel a little anxious, and that affects how we handle the call.

V: So how do you overcome this?

SS: The key to communicating well over the phone is to transmit more information.

V: How can you do that?

SS: The cold caller needs to find ways to get a conversation going by using conversation starters and, where appropriate, inject humor or some personal interest into the call as soon as possible. By doing so you inject, to some extent, emotions into your conversation, to humanize the connection and thereby create a more pleasant call experience. Remember, the person on the other end of the line is human and responds to human things. Many salespeople make the mistake of reading a script and sounding too mechanical.

V: Did you ever use a calling script for your sales calls?

SS: Absolutely! I never tried to wing it or fly by the seat of my pants when cold calling. There're too many ways to get in trouble by saying the wrong thing or not being prepared to answer a question.

V: You just said scripts were too mechanical.

SS: Stop putting shit in my mouth I didn't say. I said people who use scripts often *sound* mechanical. The first step in using a script effectively is to memorize it until it becomes second nature. The second step is to practice your responses to key questions you know you'll be asked. And finally, take those scripts and responses and make them yours.

V: What do mean?

SS: Instead of mechanically saying each word, add tone and inflection to make it sound like two guys talking on the street corner. Keep it professional, but keep it casual. You voice has to say, I'm a friend who wants to help you solve your problems. If you sound too mechanical, you'll turn the listener off and come across as telemarketer.

V: What if they're rude to you?

SS: The key is to remember that you can't control what others say, or how they say it, but you can control how you react to others. If they're rude, stay pleasant. If they're hurried, stay calm. If they're obnoxious, be patient. Don't take it personally because it isn't. If you're afraid of cold calling, your voice will reflect it over the phone. If you're unsure of yourself, your voice will reflect it over the phone. If you seem in a rush to get the call over with, your voice will reflect it over the phone.

V: So, pretty much, your attitude toward cold calling will determine your success.

SS: Yes.

V: So how do you overcome the fear? How do you get to the point where rejection doesn't sting?

SS: The only way to change our attitude about cold calling is to evaluate why we dislike it in the first place. One of my favorite authors, Ayn Rand, wrote that when it came to accepting a belief, you first had to validate it by "checking your premise." You have to go to the root of your belief system and challenge your beliefs by validating if they are true or not. By doing this, you are checking the premise of your belief system.

V: Can you explain?

SS: Assume for a moment that your belief system, your attitude towards the call, is telling you that people don't like to be interrupted.

V: Okay.

SS: Let's check the premise of that belief system. If you think people hate being interrupted, I would challenge that belief. Let's say there is a fire in the kitchen and your mother is on the phone with her best friend who she hasn't talked to in years. You know your mother hates to be interrupted while she's on the phone. Do you think she'll be mad at you for interrupting her to tell her that the house is on fire? Or do you think she'll be really mad if the house burns and you could've prevented it?

V: Of course she won't be mad if you interrupt her for something so important.

She would more likely be mad if you didn't interrupt her.

SS: So to say that people hate being interrupted is too vague and lacks context. Context is the key word here. What is the context of the interruption? If you have a great product you know will help a company save money, then people won't mind being interrupted.

V: I'd agree with that.

SS: No one in their right mind would mind being interrupted if it benefits them greatly. The value you're offering the potential client over the phone, the value of the interruption, will determine the context of the conversation. If you have great value to offer the prospect, an interruption will be welcomed. So the premise that people hate to be interrupted is false.

V: Just to reiterate, you're saying that they only hate being interrupted if you have no value to offer.

SS: If a salesperson doesn't believe in the value of what they're offering, they'll always be afraid to cold call. Do you see what I'm driving at here? This gets back to the basic premise of only selling something you believe in or not selling it at all.

V: Okay then, let me throw a couple of other fears at you, and you tell me if their premise is true.

SS: Go ahead.

V: 'Cold calling is beneath me. It sounds like I'm begging for business.' What would you say to that?

SS: First, I would say that's a sad excuse. But I would again challenge the premise. Have you ever been on a job interview?

V: Yes.

SS: Have you ever viewed that as 'begging' for a job?

V: No!

SS: If you're like most people, you see it as an exchange of value: your intelligence and capability in exchange for a salary or wage. There is no begging in this scenario; it's a necessary exchange of services for wages in a free market. This exchange on a daily basis, repeated thousands if not millions of times each day, is what makes our economy run. You following me?

V: I follow.

SS: Now let's assume you have zero skills, I mean zero! If you ask an employer for a job knowing you're not qualified and can add no value to the company, then yes, you are begging for a job. So the question you should ask yourself is, Does my product or service have value? If it does, what you seek is an exchange of your product or service for some equivalent value. This is not begging; it's business. On the flipside, if your product or service offers no value and you are trying to get someone to give you something for nothing, then you are begging. People in business are looking for an exchange of value; my product for some form of compensation. Would you agree?

V: Yes.

SS: So there is nothing about seeking an exchange of value that should make you feel like you're begging, or that it is beneath you. Begging is not an exchange or a transaction based on value. As a salesperson making a cold call, you're not looking for a handout, you're looking for an exchange.

V: Alright. I'll hit you with another one. What about those who say cold calling is a waste of time?

SS: Most people who think cold calling is a waste of time are the same folks who tried it once or twice and then gave up. Have you ever made a commitment to cold calling, let's say, 100 people with a script and then measuring the results? Most people who say it's a waste of time have never taken the time to measure how effective it could be if they just gave it a chance. Again, shift your paradigm: instead of seeing cold calling as a waste of time, let's see it as a way to generate revenue. If you knew that each time you picked up the phone you could generate a sale, would you do it?

V: Of course I would.

SS: What people are looking for is a guarantee or a high return on investment for their time invested. In cold calling, there are no guarantees. In direct marketing or advertising, there are no guarantees. No form of marketing offers a guarantee or a high return on investment.

That's reality. Go back to my example of the sack with the nine white balls and one green one. It's a numbers game, pure and simple. I was told once that 50% of sales is just showing up or being there. You can't be there if you don't reach out and make the calls.

V: Let me get back to a basic hesitation. I've often heard people say that cold calling scares them.

SS: Fear of being rejected is one of the basic causes of sales call reluctance. Every time we ask for a meeting or someone's business, we leave ourselves vulnerable to being rejected. But let's think of the good things that could happen if someone actually takes us up on our offer. Begin to see how all you need is a few "Yeses" amongst the many "Nos" to make cold calling worthwhile. Like any other activity in life where we want something from someone else, we have to ask. You can't live your life without asking for something at one time or another. Rejection and what it does to our psyche can be offset if you see selling or cold calling as a game of numbers. The more you call, the more likely your success will be. You can't be afraid of calling and being rejected. Be more afraid of never calling, never trying and never getting out of life what you can get. Your biggest fear should not be that you failed, but that you didn't even try.

V: Amen to that. Can I go back to something you mentioned earlier?

SS: Go ahead.

V: You mentioned the author Ayn Rand.

SS: Yes, what about her?

V: I get a sense you admire her.

SS: Ayn Rand was the founder of Objectivism, a philosophy for seeing things as they are and not as we would want them to be. Or as she put it, A equals A. A philosophy all salespeople, and all businesspeople for that matter, should have. So the answer is yes, I do admire her. Her philosophy made me a better salesman.

V: Can you elaborate about how it applied to helping you sell better?

SS: Rand had many philosophical nuggets that helped me navigate the emotional confusion that comes with selling. I've mentioned some already. When I talked about cold calling, I made the comment about checking your premise, a Randian rule for clear thinking. Rand says to always check the premise of any statement or remark. To do this, you should break down the statement to its irreducible primary, the base statement, and check its validity. If the statement is true, it'll withstand the scrutiny.

V: Any other nuggets?

SS: Rand talked about how every relationship should be a 'value-for-value' relationship. Every engagement or interaction should benefit both parties.

V: What if it doesn't value both sides?

SS: Then she says get the hell out of that relationship. If you think about it, it

134

works especially well in a client-salesperson relationship. If a client doesn't see the value in continuing the relationship, the client should terminate it. But if he or she is benefiting from the relationship, then it should be maintained.

V: What about from the salesman's standpoint?

SS: Same thing, quit the relationship.

V: That seems counterintuitive if you're trying to build your sales and the business.

SS: No, it isn't. Aren't there clients that can be counterproductive to growth?

V: I don't –

SS: Let me help you out. Let's say you sold a client a $100 piece of equipment. The client is so non-technical that he keeps calling you up every other day to help him work it. Every time he calls, he chews up about an hour of your time. After a week or so, you realize it's costing you more to maintain the customer than the profit you made from selling the item. In this situation, there is no longer a value-for-value relationship. The customer is getting all the value and you're losing money.

V: I guess that makes sense.

SS: You 'guess?' A friend of mine gave me a great piece of advice one time when I made the same statement. He said, "Never guess. Either you know or you don't know." So in this case, you either understood what I just said or you didn't. Which is it?

V: Yes, I understood.

SS: Have you read any of her books?

V: No.

SS: You might want to consider it. Many times have I walked into a businessman's office only to see an Ayn Rand book on the shelf. I started to notice that my best business dealings were always with people who'd read one of her books and understood the premise of value-for-value. I personally think every businessperson should read her books.

V: Any recommendations?

SS: She has so many: *Atlas Shrugged*, *The Fountainhead*, *Voice of Reason*, *For the New Intellectual*, *Capitalism: the Unknown Ideal* and many others.

V: What was your first Rand book?

SS: *For the New Intellectual*.

V: Back to cold calling. We were talking about how salespeople need to get over their fear of cold calling and how in some cases their fears are not warranted. This is where you talked about checking the premise of their fear. What happens once the call is made and they finally get someone on the line? What should they say? How about executives or managers with secretaries who are their telephone gatekeepers?

SS: Now you have to shift out of strategic mode and go into tactical mode.

136

V: Okay. Walk me through what you're thinking when you call.

SS: Before I call, I have to have an objective. Let's say that my objective is to gather information with the long-term objective of setting up a meeting.

V: Okay.

SS: If I get a gatekeeper on the phone, my objective is first to create rapport. And as we discussed, it's much more difficult because it's not a face to face encounter, so you have to listen carefully for voice tone and inflection to get an idea of what they're thinking. I always keep in mind three things: One, people like to be shown respect. Two, people like people who are cordial and friendly. And three, my favorite, people have a natural human tendency to want to help others in distress.

V: What do you mean?

SS: Have you ever asked a stranger for directions because you're lost?

V: Yes.

SS: Have you ever noticed how accommodating they are and how they stop whatever they're doing to help you?

V: Yes.

SS: Why do they stop and drop everything to help a stranger?

V: Because they're nice people.

SS: That's the easy answer, Einstein. People help, aside from being nice, because they like to demonstrate how much they know, and they also like the feeling they get from 'rescuing' others.

V: I'd agree.

SS: So I use those two components to my advantage. When I call, I'm friendly and I play the person who needs help and rescuing.

V: How?

SS: Do I have to spell everything out! When I call, I ask the gatekeeper for help. I could say something like, "Hi, I'm a little lost here and I'm hoping you could help me. I'm trying to reach Mr. X in charge of (fill in the blank), but I can't seem to reach him directly. Can you help me?" Then you go silent and wait for their response. If you say it with a smile and a warm tone, nine times out of ten you get a favorable response.

V: What if that doesn't work?

SS: In the game of human interaction, there are so many variables as to why something could work or won't work. Your job as a salesperson is to come up with as many comebacks as possible to overcome the gatekeeper.

V: I understand that, so let me pose the question another way: How did you prepare to overcome objections on the phone?

SS: Well, here's the simplest and best approach: role play. By role play, I mean go through each possible scenario in your head of how the conversation may go. If they say this, you're going to say that. I would literally sit down and write out every possible objection, and then I would write a response to overcome the objection with the goal of just getting some phone time with the mark.

V: Mark?

SS: You know, the target, the objective. The executive or manager, the mark.

V: What would you say to salespeople who say, "I don't need to role play?" Or "I don't need a script?"

SS: I'd say they're arrogant idiots waiting for an ass kicking. Soon or later, you'll step in it if you try to wing it on the phone. The best sales professionals know you can't wing it. Sometimes you only get one shot at the brass ring, and you don't want to blow it. If they're stupid enough to think they can do it without practice, then they're stupid enough to believe they'll be successful in the long run. I don't get it sometimes.

V: What about responses for overcoming objections?

SS: What about them? I practice by going over all the possible objections they can throw at me and then coming up with a response to overcome each objection. But you know what the best salespeople do that differentiates them from the pack?

V: What?

SS: They block objections before they are voiced by the client.

V: Help me understand that.

SS: Great salespeople will say something that will prevent the customer from using a specific objection. Let's say the objection that may come up is price. A good salesman will preempt the objection by saying something like, "We know our Product X is priced a bit higher than the competition, but we also know that, given our quality and support, it's actually cheaper to own our product over the long run." By making a statement like this, the salesperson has removed the objection before the objection itself has been voiced. Does that nail it for you?

V: Consider it nailed. So your objective when you encounter a gatekeeper is what?

SS: First, be the gatekeeper's friend. People will speak to people they like. People will give you access to their bosses if they like you. So build the rapport. Second is to get an opportunity to speak with the mark: the manager or executive.

V: Say you get past the gatekeeper with your charm, and overcoming of objections; then what do you do?

SS: Now the real work begins. Talking to a manager or decision maker requires that you be prepared. In other words, have your shit together before you start calling.

V: What if you're not a top executive or manager? Don't you think, for the average salesperson, it will be difficult to establish a rapport?

SS: Why?

V: Well, a top decision maker is probably looking at things from an overall company viewpoint, whereas a salesperson is just trying to sell a product or service.

SS: I've never had a problem calling top-level executives. I've never been intimidated by them either.

V: Yeah, but many would be. What do you suggest they do to overcome intimidation?

SS: The other day I was let out of my cell and allowed to go to the recreation room where they usually sit me in front of the television.

V: Did they take the straitjacket off?

SS: They never do. Unable to change the channel, I found myself watching this biography on Ron Howard, you know, Opie on *The Andy Griffith Show*.

V: Is this going somewhere?

SS: Shut up and listen. Andy Griffith came on and described how impressed he was with Ron's acting as a child. He described a particular episode where Ron as Opie was going to have to cry on screen after having killed a bird with his slingshot. They then showed the actual scene from the series. He said, "As I watched, it was obvious that Ron's pain and crying were genuine." Andy was impressed and later asked Ron how he was able to cry on cue. Ron responded by telling Andy that when the moment came to cry, he thought about his dog that had died. Andy concluded by saying, whether Ron knew it or not, that was "method acting."

V: What does this have to do with selling at the top?

SS: Everything! Method acting is the ability to empathize with the character. Decision makers don't want to talk to salespeople who don't understand what they're going through. They want to work with people who not only understand the difficulties they face in building their business, but also feel their pain. They want you to feel their sense of urgency. They want you to feel how much is at stake when they make high-risk buying decisions.

V: I know that, but how is feeling their pain going to help a person sell?

SS: As salespeople, we can't 'pretend' to understand what our customers are dealing with in order to grow their business. Showing a customer you understand their pain requires you to put yourself in their shoes. In order to sell empathetically, you must become them for the moment. In order for Ron Howard to be believable, he had to transport himself to another time and place in order to really feel the pain of losing something he loved. In business you need to take a moment to transport yourself in much the same way.

V: When do you do this?

SS: Before you make the first cold call to a customer or when you're pulling together

142

a presentation. Maybe right before you speak with the client.

V: Well, that's easier said than done. The fact is, many salespeople have never been a CEO or a key decision maker of a major company, so how can they relate? I think you being unrealistic here.

SS: You're so full of excuses, it's pathetic. If you were in sales, how would you answer these questions: Do you worry about making money?

V: Yes.

SS: Do big, high-risk decisions scare you?

V: Yes.

SS: Do you have bills to pay?

V: Of course.

SS: Have you been burned in the past when you bought something?

V: Who hasn't!

SS: Do others depend on your strength at times?

V: At times.

SS: Are decisions sometimes overwhelming when there's a lot going on?

V: Yes. I still don't see where you're going with this.

SS: Answer the question, then shut up. Do you wish someone could show you a way to do things cheaper or faster without sacrificing quality – quality of life, or product, or service?

V: Yes.

SS: You've answered yes to all these questions. Congratulations, not only are you human, but you're no different from any top-level decision maker who has the same worries. Having answered 'yes' to all the questions, you do understand and can empathize with what top decision makers deal with on a daily basis.

V: I buy what you're selling, but what happens if I still can't shake feeling intimidated?

SS: All a salesperson has to do is quietly remind himself that the person sitting across from him has problems that need to be resolved. They are looking to you, the salesperson, to provide a solution, which is why they will meet in person or speak with you over the phone. 'Method Selling' is much like method acting. Put yourself in their shoes. As you're talking to this person, get in character with them. Conjure up in your mind what it would be like to be that person in terms of responsibility.

V: So you should think about how they might be thinking and sell accordingly?

SS: You got it. Remember, their job is to increase revenue and shareholder value. Never lose sight of the obvious. As a salesperson, your job is to help, not hinder. Show these top-level executives that you have thought about their problems and have come to present some answers or solutions about how they can make or save more money.

V: Has this mindset really worked for you?

SS: Yes. Keep in mind you have to show these top executives the painful reality of not making the necessary changes by buying your products or services. You must show that it will cost them more to do nothing in the long run. Make them feel the pain of mediocrity and holding on to the status quo. But you will only be believable if you put yourself in their position, and have thought of great ways to help them, and have some facts and figures to back up your claim.

V: How do you get them to feel the pain?

SS: Well, when the directors wanted 18-month old Opie to cry, what did they do? They took away a tomahawk he had grown accustomed to holding onto. To get these top level executives 'in character' so they can feel the pain, part of your job is to show them what will happen if they don't stay current with market changes. Take away their tomahawk, their object of security, by demonstrating what their top competitors are doing or how much business or market share they're losing. Again, have statistics and market figures that support your pitch. Whatever it takes to make them feel the pain.

V: So you're saying it doesn't matter what your business is; your job is to make people feel the pain of not making a change. And you can't make them feel the pain if you don't empathize with that.

SS: Exactly. If you're selling a product or service, your job is to show others that you can solve their problems or help them move forward. This especially applies to situations where you are trying to unseat an incumbent - someone, or something, they've been buying for years. It's all about empathy, not sympathy.

V: What's the difference?

SS: Oh lord, there's a big difference. Sympathy means you understand their pain. Empathy means you feel their pain.

V: I still don't see a great difference.

SS: Your mother must be so proud of you. (In a sing-song voice) "Such a bright little boy, isn't he?"

V: Kiss off. The last thing I need is sarcasm from a guy in a padded cell with a straitjacket.

SS: Touchy, touchy. Alright, mama's boy, let me see if this will show you the difference. A man is taking a walk on the deck of a boat and sees a man bent over the railing, puking over the side, and says, "Ouch, that must hurt." That's sympathy. Now if the man walking the deck went over and starting puking with the man, that would be empathy. You see the difference?

V: In other words, I can only sympathize with you being in a straitjacket in a padded room. But if I told the guard to strap me in as well, I'd really understand you. Am I right?

SS: All you have to do is hit the button on that remote. If you asked him nicely, I'm sure he'd accommodate.

V: No thanks. I'll just have to sympathize, not empathize, with your position for now.

SS: Well said.

V: When you talk to decision makers, is there something special you do to empathize with their position?

SS: I'm a fan of reading industry magazines, websites or news in general about the industry and where it's headed. This always gave me a more rounded foundation when discussing my products and where they fit in with industry changes. Decision makers love to know that you know what's happening in the industry. They like to compare notes. All this helps in building trust and rapport.

V: Excellent point. Have you ever had a manager or executive be rude or hang up on you?

SS: It happens. I've even had decision makers set up a meeting with me at their facility and cancel while I'm waiting in the lobby. These things happen. It's part and parcel when it comes to selling. All you can do is brush yourself off and move on to the next situation.

V: Talk a little bit about conversation starters or questioning techniques over the phone.

SS: Conversation starters are a bit tougher on the phone because you may only have a few minutes to prove yourself, so I usually get to the point when calling. After a pleasant exchange, I jump right into my value proposition.

V: Tell me about that.

SS: A value proposition is the reason the other person on the phone should listen to you. When you're taking up someone's time and you want more of their time, the ultimate question in their mind is, 'What's in it for me?' The listener is thinking, 'What value can I derive from giving you my time?' You have to have a value proposition before making the call.

V: How do you go about constructing a value proposition?

SS: It all comes down to money. If I can save them money, that's great.

V: I don't know if I buy that. Some customers may not be concerned about a better price; maybe they want better service.

SS: It comes down to money no matter how you slice it. If I can save them time, that translates into money. If I can offer them better service, which saves them time, that translates into money. If they find my product easier to use, that means less training, thereby saving them more money. The value proposition is really a money proposition in disguise.

V: How do you craft one?

SS: A value proposition?

V: Yes.

SS: You have to figure out what your customer's hot buttons are. Is he concerned about product price? Ease of use? Long-term costs associated with owning the product? Training? Support? You have to find out what the itch is, and then you scratch it.

V: How do you go about finding out?

SS: I believe in the golden rule that if you're asking the questions, then you're in control of the conversation. This is key.

V: So you fire questions at the client?

SS: No, you don't fire questions at someone, or it becomes an interrogation. We've had this conversation already. You have to ask polite, open-ended questions.

V: Open-ended questions as opposed to close-ended questions?

SS: Close-ended questions will always elicit a one-word answer from the client. I try to avoid these. Open-ended questions require the client to elaborate or explain their position. Within these explanations are the seeds of successful selling. The more a customer opens up, the more you begin to get a sense of what's bothering them or what they're looking for.

V: So they're telling you how to sell them.

SS: Exactly. The more we know their pain, the better we can position our product or service to remove that pain. The trick is getting the customer to 'open up his kimono.'

V: Kimono?

SS: Just a figure of speech meaning get the customer to reveal what's really bothering him or her. The more you gain their trust, the more they'll reveal.

V: How do you gain trust?

SS: Not easily. Many clients are jaded from having been burned in the past by salespeople who oversold their product or service, so you're always dealing with a skeptical client right off the bat. The trick to gaining some semblance of trust upfront is not to be too pushy and not seem overly anxious to win the client's business.

V: What's wrong with showing them that you want their business?

SS: Nothing. But you have to be careful not to come across as desperate, either. Sometimes when you push too hard, you push the client away. The best way to sell is to pull the client in by offering compelling reasons why they might want to do business with you.

V: We're back to the value proposition.

SS: I believe the best way to sell is to pull a customer in, not push them into buying. Never try to sell them on the first call. The first call is a reconnaissance call to get information or as much G2 as you can.

V: G2?

SS: Military lingo for gather information. The real goal is to set up a follow-up meeting face to face to discuss in detail how you can help the client. The phone call is merely a tool to gather information which you will then use later to present and convince the client that they should be doing business with you.

V: So then you have to make a choice before you call. You're either gathering intelligence or presenting a value proposition.

SS: Yes. So unless you know the client well already, you would be doing the former, not the latter.

V: So then I would gather as much information as possible upfront and then work to set up a meeting to present a value proposition?

SS: Yes.

V: What type of G2 should I be gathering?

SS: A lot of things. You want to know upfront if they're even interested in the product. What are they using at the moment? Who's your competition? How much have they paid in the past? Is your price too high? Do they have a budget for this year to buy your product if they wanted? Are they happy with their current supplier? If not, why not? If so, why? Answers to these questions are critical for the follow-up presentation. You have to find subtle ways to pose these questions without making it seem like you're pumping them for information. Nothing shuts down a conversation faster than when the other person feels like they're being squeezed for information. Again, it's not an interrogation, it's a conversation. The best salespeople know how to gather information without being so obvious about their intent.

V: I got it. You've driven the point home quite nicely regarding interrogation versus conversation. Let's move the process one step ahead and assume we made initial contact, gathered the required information and secured a follow-up meeting. Walk through the process of preparing and presenting the value proposition. How did you do it? What are some of the things salespeople should look out for?

SS: Before we go there, I want to point out that sometimes the objective can be to find out that maybe this isn't the right customer for you.

V: You lost me.

SS: As you're gathering information, you may discover that this isn't a good prospect. Maybe they don't have a budget to buy anything this year. Maybe they've just purchased a similar product, so they won't be buying for another year. My point is, sometimes you're there not to secure a presentation, but to qualify the client to see if it's worth a follow-up meeting. So you're not spinning your wheels.

V: Got it. Let's assume that it's a qualified client based on your initial conversation. What then?

SS: Well, if the client agrees to a meeting, the next thing is to ensure that all the decision makers are in the room. One of the biggest mistakes you can make is to have a meeting and not have the key decision makers there, especially if the decision requires the involvement of multiple departments.

V: Why?

SS: Every sale is complex, with many moving parts and players. When a client who wasn't a CEO or president told me they were the sole decision maker, I didn't buy it. Many key players in a company will lie to you and tell you they make all the decisions. I never bought it. It's rare that there is only one decision maker, very rare.

V: What did you do to make sure the decision makers were in the room?

SS: The first thing to do is understand who's involved and how the decision process works.

V: But how do you get others to show up when you've just met the decision maker over the phone?

SS: You have to find ways to work the question in as to who should be attending the meeting. For example, you can simply ask, "Who else should attend this meeting that would be part of the decision making process?" Or you can flat out ask, "Are you the sole decision maker or will others have to be involved?" If the response is that others have to be involved, you can ask, "Is it possible to have them at the meeting as well?" There are so many ways to pose the question, it's a matter of finding a polite and low-key way of asking without coming across as pushy.

V: Easier said than done.

SS: You're right. There's no set formula for how you do it. It's all about timing and finesse. You have to find the right moment during the conversation to slip those questions in or simply encourage the client to invite others who may be involved to the meeting.

V: Fair enough. So what was your strategy once you got everyone in the room who could make a decision?

SS: Then it's time for the dog and pony show.

V: What's that?

SS: We call all presentations or demonstrations in front of a customer a 'dog and pony show.' This is where we put our best foot forward by pulling together a presentation that shows off the company's strengths.

V: How do you pull a presentation together? What do you do? Doesn't it make you nervous knowing the decision makers are in the room?

SS: Whoa! One at a time. Yes, I'm always a bit nervous, but not like I was when I first started. Back then, I felt like puking right before I went in to do the presentation.

V: How did you cure that?

SS: When you first do a presentation, you're going to be nervous because you have to worry about two things. The first is that you have to remember everything important and relevant about the product you're presenting. Missing a key feature or not highlighting a benefit could cost you the sale.

V: And the second thing?

SS: The second thing that made me nervous was not knowing what types of questions were going to be asked. I remember always reading my notes, re-reading the brochures and anything about our product to prepare for the meeting. But always, I mean *always*, there was that one person who was ahead of the curve, who would ask that one question I didn't see coming.

V: What do you do?

SS: You do the only thing you can do – admit you don't know the answer, write it down right there and then, and promise the questioner you'll get back to them with an answer.

V: Did this kill your presentation?

SS: It depends on the strength or relevancy of the question. If it was one of those deal breaker questions, then the answer is yes, it hurt. Not being able to answer the question right there, with all the decision makers, is always a black mark. Because even if you got back to them by writing an e-mail, the impact of the response is gone and you're never sure if the decision makers will read your response. If they were looking for a way to say 'no,' they could use this one issue as an excuse to turn you down. It's a very tricky business, presenting.

V: Does it get easier with time?

SS: It only gets easier in the sense that, as you do more and more presentations, you begin to know the product's hot buttons, and you've also heard almost any question that could possibly be asked. So it's rare that you're caught off guard. In this sense, it does get easier to execute a great presentation. So, if you're just starting out, the best way to prepare is to create a list of possible objections. A list of every possible objection someone in the room would raise as an excuse not to do business with you.

V: How?

SS: Like I said earlier about how I prepare before calling a prospect, I role play in my head what the objections may be. But in this case, as I'm doing a presentation, I insert the possible objection and then overcome it by explaining how our product or service addresses that concern.

V: In other words, as you're doing a presentation, you bring up an objection and then dismiss it by addressing it directly. Give me an example.

SS: Let's take the common objection of price again. I will admit that our products are typically, let's say, 20 percent higher than our competitors' but that the cost of ownership over time is cheaper because we have fewer problems with the product. Or if a product doesn't have a certain feature they want, you can acknowledge that the feature doesn't exist today, but in another X months it will be available. See what I mean?

V: But isn't bringing up a weakness a bad thing?

SS: People today are smart. They'll figure it out eventually. The Internet has made gathering information on a company and its product very easy. In the old days, before the Internet, the seller could control the information. Today, it's a free-for-all.

V: I agree, but still, why bring up a problem or a weakness?

SS: I learned many years ago that if you bring it up, you own it. If they bring it up, you're defending and explaining - not a good position to be in.

V: Why? Why not explain your position if they bring it up?

SS: Another lessoned I learned is that if you find yourself in a position where you're explaining, you're losing the conversation. That's been a valuable business axiom for me. I never want to be in a position where I'm defending or explaining my position. If you find yourself in this position, the chances of making a sale go down, and the chances of saying something stupid go up.

V: What are some strategies or techniques you use during a presentation that you'd say are highly effective?

SS: A presentation is really a sequence of mini-presentations. Each mini-presentation is aimed at answering a question in the customer's mind, or diffusing a concern. You asked earlier about the value proposition. The value proposition itself is the sum total of all these mini-presentations. The goal is to create enough interest and momentum during the presentation that a customer will want to take the next step, whatever that may be.

V: So a question left unanswered is a momentum-killer.

SS: Took you a while, but you're getting it. Every question – in fact, *any* question – left unanswered creates a sort of 'decision friction' whereby the customer will not want to take the next step, depending on the question. The only thing you can do as a salesperson is prepare, prepare and prepare some more. But only time and experience will allow you to get to the level of a flawless presentation.

V: Practice, practice, practice.

SS: You got it. There is no shortcut.

V: Let's go back and discuss some of your techniques and strategies when you present.

SS: I treat a presentation like a conversation in the sense that I try not to sound canned or as if I had done this presentation a thousand times. Always try to sound natural and come across as believable and genuine.

V: I once heard that it's best not to let people ask questions during a presentation; what do you say?

SS: It depends on the venue and who you're speaking to. I, personally, never let people ask me questions until I'm ready to take them.

V: Really! Why is that?

SS: Well, first, the question most likely will be answered during the course of the conversation. If the question is brought up earlier, I would then have to stop and explain it.

V: What's wrong with that?

SS: Sometimes you need to cover specific material before you can answer the question. You have to educate them on certain aspects of your product or service first before they can understand the answer to the question. If the question is brought up too early, you're caught.

SS: What do you do?

V: I politely tell them that their questions will be answered in the next few minutes, and I stress how I need to cover a few more things before I answer the question.

V: Does that usually work?

SS: Nine times out of ten, if not more. The other reason I don't like to answer questions is that sometimes the audience member will ask a question that is tangential to what we're talking about.

V: The question has little or nothing to do with what you're presenting.

SS: Yeah. Sometimes it could be one of those minutiae questions that isn't pertinent to the discussion.

V: Is that irritating?

SS: Only if the questioner demands an answer or keeps coming back to it. And yes, that does happen. Welcome to Sales Presentation 101.

V: What's your presentation structure?

SS: I follow the tried and true rule: Tell them what you're going to tell them, then tell them, and at the end, remind them what you just told them. The last part is key; always do a recap and tell them what you've just told them.

V: Is that necessary?

SS: Absolutely! You'd be amazed at what people miss during a presentation. Summarizing your key points at the end is crucial to maintaining the momentum to take it to the next step.

V: Okay. Let's say the presentation went well, and they want you to come back to do a follow-up presentation or have you submit a proposal, or whatever the case may be. What I'd like to know is, how do you keep the momentum up from a relationship standpoint?

SS: I don't understand the question.

V: Say your presentation was right on the money. They say they'd like to do a follow-up meeting after they've had a chance to review the proposal in detail. What do you do then? Do you sit back and wait? What?

SS: I got it. (pause) Let me think for a second.

V: Take your time.

SS: I mean, it really depends on the situation. I always ask if there is one person that could serve as a contact point for the company. I think this is very important and telling.

V: What do you mean?

SS: Alright, the presentation is over and it went extremely well. They want some time to review the proposal and then get back to me. I would ask, in a roundabout way, when is the best time to get back to them. They'll typically respond with some vague answer like "Sometime next week." To which I always say okay and then ask if there is one person I can call to get a status report. Without fail, the group would assign a point man or woman that I could call to get an update. This, to me, was very important.

V: Why? So you can get an update?

SS: No, you shit. Think. If they choose a person to be my point of contact, that tells me this person has some type of status within the group, or why else would they assign him or her the task.

Transcript Note > Interviewee discusses using entertainment as a way of getting information.

V: So you know the point of contact. Would you call him?

SS: Hell, I'd not only call him, I'd see if I could invite him out to lunch. If I could get him out to lunch, I could use that time to pump him for some information or insight.

V: Like what?

SS: Damn, amigo, you sure are slow on the uptake. During the lunch, I'd ask him about what the group thought of the presentation, what was some of the feedback, were there any other companies bidding for the business, and more. My goal was to get as much G2 as I could, to see whether or not I stood a good chance of winning the business.

V: Did clients accept your lunch invitation?

SS: What do you think? In most cases they said yes. Who could say no to a free lunch?

V: Why not dinner?

SS: Oh no, dinner was the second step. Accepting a dinner invitation was code for "We really want to do business with you." If I could get them to go to dinner, then I was sure I was on the right track.

V: I've heard wild stories of salespeople taking clients out to a golf course or some late-night entertainment spot.

SS: Whatever the customer wants. If they wanted to go golfing, I took them. If they wanted to visit some late-night spot, I took them.

V: Did you pay for this?

SS: Absolutely.

V: Wasn't that expensive?

SS: Oh yeah, it got expensive, but if I won the deal, the cost would be minimal in comparison. If you're going after big sales, be prepared to spend big money. I've had clients specifically request that I take them to some seedy night spot to watch strippers.

V: Did you take them?

SS: I'm not judge or jury. If a potential customer wanted to go to strip joint, I was more than happy to accommodate the request.

V: You didn't have moral dilemma?

SS: Hell, no. If anything, here's what I've discovered: Going to a strip joint with a client is a bonding experience. If I could get a customer to a strip joint, per their request, my chances of closing the deal just went up!

V: Really?

SS: You bet your ass.

V: Out of curiosity, how did you pay for this? I'm sure a company would never pick up the tab for a strip joint.

SS: You're right. God bless taxi receipts. You may not be able to get reimbursed for a lap dance, but you can always get reimbursed for a taxi ride.

V: Are you saying you buried the cost by padding taxi receipts?

SS: Companies would never condone it, but they never discourage it either. At least I'm not a hypocrite about it.

V: Sounds like a hard way to make a sale.

SS: I'm sure there was no pun intended. Hey, life's a bitch; I just try to make things work so I don't miss out on an opportunity to sell and make money. I go where the deals lead me. It's the only way to get big.

V: So you like to do things big?

SS: I once heard the phrase, 'Think big, be big; think small, stay small.' You can't shrink away from success. If business is done at a golf course, I'm there. If it's done at a strip joint, I'm there. I'm wherever the client is ready to make a deal.

V: You make sales sound like a whore's game?

SS: Judge all you want, but the answer is yes. The whore sells what he or she has out of necessity, and the one thing the whore will never sell is his or her soul; sales is no different. We sell out of necessity; the trick is to do so without selling yourself out. Does that answer your question, moralizing son of a bitch?

V: I'm not judging, I'm just posing the question.

SS: Bullshit! I could hear the indignation in your tone; don't try to hide it. Here's what you're not getting, and I think it's crucial that you understand this subtle point: When you mingle with people outside of work, over time you establish this relationship that moves beyond rapport. When you share experiences with someone else - be it at the golf course, a casino, strip joint, dinner or an innocent trip to Disney - you now have a shared experience that you can use as a reference point. Maybe the next time you talk, you begin by reminiscing about the great time you had. These shared moments over time help develop a trust and a bond between the client and you. You're not just there to sell them once, you're there to build a relationship to sell them repeatedly over time. Having shared experiences gives you both an opportunity to get to know each other. It's all about building trust and, hopefully, a mutually beneficial friendship with the client. Does that make sense, or am I just blowing in the wind?

V: I understand.

SS: You understand.

V: Yes, I get it. So let me push this conversation to the next logical step in the sales process, money. Let's say you've got the customer hooked, and he now wants to negotiate price. What's your strategy there?

SS: Alright. First, we have to assume we've gotten to the point that the customer has asked for some type of pricing and proposal. Putting a sales proposal together is another art form onto itself. You have to be careful how you present price. If you present the price before creating the value, the client will see it as too expensive. On the flip side, if you price your product too low, the client may wonder why and think that your product has some type of defect, or why else would you price it so low.

V: I see the dilemma. So what do you do?

SS: Not so fast. We also have to take into account that the customer wants to think they're getting a great deal. We also know that any client worth his salt is going to ask you for some type of price break, especially now that you've bonded at some social event and the relationship has moved forward.

V: It's psychologically messy.

SS: Yes, there are many emotional dynamics to consider. Which is why the proposal has to be crafted carefully. The first assumption I make is that no customer wants to pay list price or the going rate for your product or service. They expect a better deal, or why else would they spend time with you.

V: Wait a minute. You're saying a customer will agree to spend time with you so that they can get a better deal?

SS: Your naïveté never ceases to fucking amaze. Of course the client is looking for the angle as well. A customer will spend time with you to pump *you* for information and, if they want to buy from you, to get a better price. I mean, come on, you would never charge a friend list price. The entertainment excursions are like mating rituals where you try to impress the other and hopefully find some advantage.

V: I take it this goes back to the mutually beneficial relationship equation?

SS: Damn right. So in a proposal, you can't charge your friend list price; they expect a discount of some sort. I typically start out with a standard discount, knowing full well that I will probably have to lower my price even more. So if the standard discount is 25%, then I start by quoting a 15% discount. As the negotiation progresses, I can then use the remaining 10% to solidify or, better said, close the deal.

V: You don't mind lowering your prices?

SS: I hate lowering my prices. I hate giving away discounts. I hate giving away large discounts in particular, because that means in the long run I have to sell more products just to make up for that discount.

V: So what's the best defense against discounting prices?

SS: There are a couple of defensive strategies. One, you have to level set your client by telling him in so many words that he's getting a good deal compared to what's out in the marketplace. You can tell him how your product has so many bells and whistles that it really is a great price.

V: Does that usually work?

SS: Eh, it's hit or miss depending on the situation. The second strategy is to really build the value of the company and how you'll support his products over time.

V: Any other strategies?

SS: You could try the riskiest of them all – but it's risky. You can use the 'defer to the higher authority' move.

V: What's that?

SS: You can tell your client that you've gone as low as you can. You also tell him that you went to your superior and begged, I mean really begged, for a better price, but you were shut down and there's nothing you can do about it.

V: Will a client go for this?

SS: Sure. It's an effective strategy to stave off any more requests for discounts, but again, it may also turn the client off. The only way to avoid this is to really beat the client over the head with the features and, more importantly, the benefits of buying from you. If you can do this, you have just created a very compelling value proposition. Not only are you offering a great price for a great product, you're also offering something a lot of clients value: service.

V: Service is hard to quantify.

SS: Yes, it is. That's why building a relationship based on mutual trust is important. The client will judge not only the product, but more importantly the type of service he or she can expect, by the type of salesperson you are. Are you warm, open, trustworthy? Do you follow through on things you promised to do? Did you arrive on time for the meeting? Were you well prepared? A salesperson is judged on all the little things he or she does, which to the customer represents a summary of the type of relationship he can expect if he buys from your company. When you're in sales, you are always going to be judged by a client. Does that make sense?

V: Makes perfect sense. Well said.

SS: Another thing to keep in mind is that once you give a discount, you have to make it up elsewhere.

V: What do you mean?

SS: If I give a 20% discount, that means my sales figure is 20% lower, which means I have to make it up somewhere else.

V: You mean, in order to meet your sales quota?

SS: Yep. That's why I'm always reluctant to give a discount. And here's one more thing about discounts. If a buyer doesn't buy from me because of price, then that only tells me that the salesperson, in this case me, didn't create enough value in the value proposition during the presentation.

V: Let's go back and talk about the dog and pony show and how you give presentations.

170

SS: Every presentation has to have an objective. In most cases, it's to convince the client that your company offers a superior product or service.

V: I got that. Let's get to some of your tactics for convincing a client to move in your direction.

SS: Alright, don't rush me, I'm getting there. I'll start by saying that the most valuable lesson I learned is that during any presentation, it's okay to let your personality show through a bit.

V: Be yourself?

SS: Yes. It seems obvious but many salespeople try to sound too professional and they wind up sounding like a canned commercial.

V: What's wrong with that?

SS: Again, people buy from people they like and can relate to. They want to get to know you; it's about building personal rapport. People want not only to buy from you, they want to establish a long-term working relationship. But if you sound like a machine or automaton, spewing out a sales script, it doesn't help in most circumstances.

V: When does it ever help to sound like an automaton?

SS: When you're selling to the government! (Laughs)

V: You're a funny guy. Anything else on presentations?

SS: The most important part of any presentation is making sure the customer understands the full value of what you bring to the table.

V: I want to go back to something you said earlier about not taking questions during the presentation. Do you wait till the end and do a question and answer session?

SS: Yes. But let me take a step back as well and explain what's behind my strategy when it comes to presenting. All my presentations have built into them all the most common questions asked by a client. So as I go through the presentation, I'm conscious of making sure to emphasize the answers to those questions. Now, not only will the client have questions, they will also have what I call silent objections.

V: Silent objections are ...

SS: These are objections that are never voiced during a presentation. I've noticed over the years that it's not what people say that can kill a deal, it's what they don't say that can hurt you. Silent objections are deadly deal killers because you never hear them; therefore, you can't address them.

V: Why do think these objections aren't brought to the surface and discussed?

SS: When you have a group, I think it all comes down to not wanting to look stupid. When you get more than two people in a room, I've noticed that the number of questions will be lower. Most clients don't want to ask questions in front of their colleagues for fear of being seen as incompetent or not as bright; so they keep those objections to themselves. These are silent deal killers.

V: What is the difference between a question and objection, if there is one?

SS: A question is aimed at getting clarification. An objection is a challenge to a claim you've made, or why they don't want to buy from you.

V: Got it.

SS: Again, I try to answer as many questions as I can about the product or service. The real art of presentation is knowing how to not only answer anticipated questions, but to prevent objections from creeping into the client's mind.

V: Give me an example.

SS: Well, we talked about it a bit earlier, but here's a similar example. Let's say the objection that they voice or think of voicing is that the price of the product is too high. In the presentation, I would say something like, "A lot of people think our prices are higher and they would be right." This statement confuses or stuns the client momentarily and grabs their attention. They're thinking, "This guy just admitted that the price is too high. I knew it!" I then say something like, "The reason our prices are a bit higher is because we offer X, Y and Z, which our competitors either don't offer or would charge you more for, if you wanted them." Do you see what I did?

V: I do. You raised an objection, and then you clarified it to remove the objection from the client's mind.

SS: Yeah. It gets the client to think, "Oh, that makes sense." Or "That explains why it's higher." The client can now be re-engaged in the presentation instead of being preoccupied with the thought of why is this product so expensive. You can also do this with product features. If your product doesn't have a certain feature your competitor is using, you can raise the objection and then dismiss it using one of two strategies: Let them know that the feature will be incorporated in the next few months, years or whatever, or tell them the reason the feature isn't included is because we've found that it's unnecessary or slows down the system or .... Either way, you've brought up the objection and explained it away.

V: Wait. What if the feature is critical and you don't offer it?

SS: You can either walk away from the sale if it's a deal killer, or you can tell them that it will be incorporated at a later date. If they can't wait, you're pretty much S.O.L.

V: Shit out of luck?

SS: Yeah.

V: Give me another example of objection blocking.

SS: Uh, how about when a client says I don't have the money or it's not in my budget. Should you believe them?

V: Is there a reason not to?

SS: Yes. Most people think that, second only to lawyers, the biggest liars in business are salespeople. I would challenge that by telling you that clients can be the biggest liars; they're not always being 100% truthful with you.

V: Why would a customer lie when they're in the driver's seat?

SS: It could be that they don't want to tip me off as to how they're really leaning. Maybe they're holding back because they can't make the decision – because they're not the decision maker. It may be because they're considering other offers and don't want me to know about it. There could be a variety of reasons, and my job was to dig and uncover those reasons. I did that by getting them to voice their objections through clever questioning. If the issue was price, for example, I would challenge that excuse, because the way I see it, in any transaction someone is being sold. Either you sell them or they'll sell you.

V: I'm not sure I get it.

SS: Look, either you'll sell them on the fact that the objection they've raised is flimsy or an excuse not to get started, or they'll sell you on the excuse being valid. They will try to sell you on the idea that they don't have the financial resources. I would argue and sell them on the idea that it would be a good financial investment that would save them money in the long run, not cost them money. Either way, someone is getting sold in this deal: them or me. I prefer it be them.

V: I see.

SS: In a presentation, you have to make sure that objections are addressed and put to bed. Again, I pepper my presentation with objection blockers to remove any excuse the client may think of for not buying from me.

V: Anything else?

SS: One last thing. Before doing any type of presentation, research your competitors and identify their weaknesses so that you can highlight them. I believe strongly in the philosophy of sewing as much discontent as I can when it comes to my clients who are complacent or content with the status quo.

V: Explain.

SS: Say you're trying to sell a product to a client who already has a similar product, albeit inferior, and the client is using that as an excuse for not buying from you. If I know the competitor's product, I will drop little seeds of discontent throughout the discussion. For example, if the competitor product doesn't have a particular feature, I'll go out of my way to emphasize that our product has it and make light mention that our competitor's doesn't.

V: So you badmouth your competition?

SS: No, no, no! Never badmouth your competition, because it never does you any good. In fact, it will cast a shadow of mistrust if you do.

V: How so?

SS: The clients will first see your bashing as unprofessional. Customers want to do business with professionals. The client may also see your badmouthing as insecurity on your part and become suspicious.

V: Suspicious?

SS: You know, they're going to start thinking to themselves, "Why is he so bent on badmouthing this competitor? Maybe I should dig into this a little further." Your negativity will plant a seed of doubt, and doubt is an objection in disguise. Which brings up a very good point: never mention your competition by name.

V: Never?

SS: Never. I once made this mistake when I started selling. I casually made a comment that our product was better than ABC Competitor's. One of the audience members responded, "Who's ABC? We've never heard of them." At that moment, I was done. Not only did I just introduce them to my competition, they also weren't going to decide to buy from me until they checked out what ABC Competitor had to offer. In other words, I shot myself in the foot by mentioning them. So I suggest that if you want to be a great salesperson, don't mention the competition by name, but do drop seeds of discontent during the presentation by highlighting your features and added value, and then let them draw the conclusion about who's a better company.

V: So I take it you not only study your own product but your competitors' products as well?

SS: (Laughing menacingly) That's what Serial Sellers do!

V: Funny guy.

SS: Couldn't resist. I should add that one of things I always look for in an audience is a sympathetic ally, someone who likes what they're hearing.

V: You mean you're looking for someone to champion your product?

SS: Good boy! It's critical, *critical*, to find someone in the company who will talk up your product when you're not there. If you can find this person, you'll be one step ahead of the competition.

V: Do they have to be a person with authority?

SS: Yes and no.

V: Clarify, please.

SS: Yes, if you can find a person who has authority, that's great. If you can get the president or the CEO to be your champion, you're 'in like Flynn.' But position isn't power. There are people who may be low on the organization chart, yet have substantial influence. What you're looking for are people who have the power to influence. Would you agree that there is a difference?

V: Yes.

SS: So we're also looking for who has influence.

V: How do you find them if you can't look at an organization chart?

SS: Use your judgment; that's what makes a great salesperson. Have the presence of mind during a presentation or a meeting to distinguish, in the room, who's a player and who isn't. Organization charts don't mean shit. Forget the lines written on it; look for the informal lines. In other words, during a meeting or presentation, there may be one or two people asking the real tough questions or taking voracious notes. Look for the person who's leaning forward, listening attentively to your presentation. Look for the person everyone seems to glance at when something important is said.

V: Why is that?

SS: A person of influence is someone whose opinion others respect. When something is said that is controversial, challenging or simply new, others will usually look at a person of power to gauge their reaction, because they themselves have no way of knowing whether what was just said is a good thing or a bad thing. People of influence don't usually look to others for validation.

V: You said you never like for people to ask questions. If so, how can you determine the influencers?

SS: Always, at the end of any meeting, there is a question and answer session. That's when those who are really there to determine whether or not to buy from you will begin asking questions.

V: Has it ever happened that they *don't* ask questions at the end?

SS: Yes. I've never found that to be a good thing.

V: Why? I think you would want that.

SS: Quite the contrary. I prefer a lot of questions, because it tells me the audience is fully engaged and there to make a decision. The quality, not quantity, of questions is a good indicator that you've done well. The tougher, more in-depth and insightful the questions, the better for you; that means they really want to know more about your product or service. If at the end of the presentation you had few or no questions, that to me always indicated a sense of apathy and indifference to what was presented, and that's not good. You want questions raised so you can answer or clarify them, so there are no misunderstandings once you leave.

V: Has that ever happened? Misunderstandings?

SS: I've done presentations where I've reiterated a certain point but, for some reason or another, the client still got it wrong. And because they got it wrong, my proposal was dismissed. It happens, and the best you can do is make sure during the question and answer session that your main points are restated.

V: What happens when you lose a deal? What do you do when you've been beaten by a competitor?

SS: First, lick your wounds. Second, call the client and find out why you lost. And lastly, move on to the next client and don't take it personally.

V: You call the client to ask why you weren't chosen?

SS: Absolutely! That's the best intelligence you can get. Once a decision is made, I've noticed that clients are more than willing to tell you why you lost the deal. They don't feel restrained in telling you flat-out what happened; they will be brutally honest. And when you do call to ask what happened, your tone mustn't be defensive or angry. If it is, they won't be as open for fear of provoking a confrontation where they'll have to defend their decision.

V: Should you try to convince them to reconsider?

SS: No. That strategy is futile.

V: Why?

SS: It's a bit complicated to explain, but it comes down to defending a decision that's already been made. Have you ever noticed that once you've made a decision to buy something, you will then look for reasons to reaffirm your decision? People, when they buy something, look for reasons after the fact to justify their decision, and they will block out any reasons to the contrary. So even if you present new information, it doesn't matter: the decision has been made. When I first started in sales, I would try to convince the client of their error, and often times the tone of the conversation would turn negative. I realized quickly I was shooting myself in the foot.

V: Why?

SS: Well, because people don't like to talk to people they don't like or have some issue with. By arguing with my client, I created an environment where it became uncomfortable for them to work with me. So when the next opportunity came around to do business with them, I wasn't invited to present my proposal. I learned never to argue when you lose a deal. Simply follow up, find out why, learn from it and move on to the next deal.

V: I believe that's called wisdom.

SS: Yes. Wish I'd had more of it when I first started out.

V: I think this is a good place to stop our interview. But I have one final question which you said you'd answer at the end.

SS: What was that?

V: At the beginning, you refused to talk about your father when I asked how he influenced you as a person and how that may have molded you into a Serial Seller.

SS: You have a good memory, I'll grant you that.

V: So are you ready to discuss him now? Remember our agreement, no holding back.

SS: You've put me in a very uncomfortable position.

V: Why is that?

SS: You're asking me to summarize a man's life and his impact in a short span of time, and no matter what I say, I can never do him justice.

V: I understand, but try anyway.

SS: My father came to this country, like many others, with little or no education. He worked in a job he hated. He raised a family and never complained. He was a kind and generous man who treated his children well. He would lend people a hand when he could. And he never cheated anyone. So what did he teach me by example? He taught me that a good education is important. We take for granted our ability to educate ourselves, not knowing there are millions of people out there who have no education and would literally give their right arms to have access to the information and education we take for granted. This may explain why I think continuous learning and being the best at your trade are key elements of sales success. My father hated his job, yet he busted his ass to support his family. What did this teach me? First, find a job that you enjoy doing. If you love sales, then the second task is to find something you enjoy selling. There's no point in making money if you hate what you're doing. Sooner or later, the money won't be enough to soothe the pain of discontent that builds when we're out of sync with our own desires. I never heard my father complain about how hard his job was. I don't think he had a choice when it came to where he worked, because he had limited skills. Today, our potential to do what we want to do is limited only by our own imagination. I mentioned earlier that I don't believe in loyalty but rather a value-for-value relationship with a company. Unless there's a win-win, I don't see any point in maintaining the relationship. My father was trapped. After twenty-plus years of working with one company, the only thing he got was a nice slap on the back and some chump change as a thank you for all those years of service. This taught me that no one will look out for you, until you learn to look out for yourself. This doesn't mean you take advantage of others; it means you take care of yourself first. My father never complained about working hard to support his family. He never bitched about what we didn't have or, more importantly, what he didn't have because he was feeding so many mouths. He taught me the meaning of responsibility: never whine about the decisions you've made, just do what's right and shut up. My father was a kind man who treated people with respect and dignity. I never heard him yell at anyone and I never saw him refuse a favor he could grant. He taught me that being kind is a good thing, and he taught me through his actions never to take advantage of other people. In the game of sales, there are many ways to go astray if you let the money influence you. I've seen it happen. Time has taught me that there are no shortcuts, and what goes around does indeed have a way of coming back to bite you in the ass. I don't like looking over my shoulder, which is why I always try to do right by my clients by giving them all the information they need, without hype or exaggeration, for them to make a good business decision. I never knew my father to cheat anyone in order to get what he wanted. I'd rather lose a deal or lose a client before being accused misleading or misinforming someone. The cost of selling one's soul in business is high, and I'm not willing to pay it. So there you have it. Did that answer your question?

V: Yes. Yes, it does. Thank you for being candid and thank you for your time.

SS: My pleasure. On the way out, don't forget to put in a good word for me with the warden.

V: I'll see what I can do.